IMPROVE YOUR
SQUASH

IMPROVE YOUR SQUASH

Willow Books
Collins
8 Grafton Street, London W1
1988

Willow Books
William Collins Sons & Co Ltd
London · Glasgow · Sydney · Auckland
Toronto · Johannesburg

First published 1988
© William Collins Sons & Co Ltd 1988

BRITISH LIBRARY CATALOGUING IN PUBLICATION DATA
Improve your squash.
1. Squash rackets – Manuals
796.34'3

ISBN 0-00-218302-1

Designed by Sackville Design Group Ltd
Hales Barn, New Street, Stradbroke, Suffolk IP21 5JG
Editorial consultant: Colin McQuillan
Art director: Al Rockall
Art editor: Joyce Chester
Editor: Lorraine Jerram
Diagrams: David Cringle
Set in Melior by Bookworm Typesetting, Manchester
Printed and bound in Italy by New Interlitho S.P.A. Milan

Contents

Winning squash

Some might think that being a professional takes away some of the excitement of playing a sport. My own experience, however, contradicts such a view, and this, I believe, is due mainly to the fact that squash is a game of such vast potential. Not only is there immense satisfaction to be derived from competing and from winning, but this satisfaction increases the more physical effort you make. Even at this stage of my career, when the novelty of competition has to some extent worn off, there is still so much to be gained from playing on the circuit. Not least among these pleasures is the chance to travel and meet other sportsmen and women worldwide, for squash is a truly international sport.

Although my development as a player is not perhaps typical, it may serve as an encouragement to anyone taking up the game who is determined to achieve their ambitions, whatever those may be. I first began playing squash as a hobby and soon realized, at the age of about twelve, that I was a fairly good player. Steady progress and no little success persuaded me to turn professional in January 1980, at the age of twenty. However, it took a dramatic, and nearly catastrophic, event in 1983 to spur me on to the greatest victory of my career. The turning-point was a parachuting accident which could easily have meant the end of my playing days.

During the nine months' recovery period, I learnt more about squash than at any other time. This new understanding enabled me to formulate clear goals and to sharpen my determination not only to regain fitness but, above all, to succeed. I also developed that all-important element of self-belief, without which I would not have been able to achieve my greatest ambition: to beat Jahangir Khan. This victory, in November 1986, which brought to an end Jahangir's five-and-a-half year undefeated reign, was the high-point of my career, the culmination of intense mental and physical preparation. It sometimes happens in squash, as in other sports, that everything comes right on the day, and this was just such an occasion.

For me, one of the attractions of the sport is that it teaches discipline, both mental and physical. However, people have many different reasons for wanting to play, and squash certainly caters for a wide range of tastes and requirements. Equally as encouraging as the number of youngsters taking up the sport is the growing participation of 'older' players – the veteran and vintage categories are very well represented nowadays. Similarly, it is extremely pleasing to see the women's game developing alongside the men's; this is essential for the healthy growth of the sport as a whole.

As a means of maintaining fitness and having fun at the same time, squash is second to none. It can be played by everyone and is easy to take up; it has become much more accessible due to the growing number and quality of the courts available; it is an action-packed sport with a quick result, so can be played during lunch hours or after work; it is mentally as well as physically stimulating; and, unlike tennis, the ball rarely goes out, so you can keep playing for longer periods! These are just some of the reasons why squash has really taken off all over Europe and why it is gaining a strong foothold in the United States, where it looks poised to replace the hardball game.

Another reason for the growing popularity of the sport is the vast improvements that have been made over the last few years in the area of television coverage. Special futuristic all-glass showcourts have been built, and 'teleballs' with reflective inserts designed, for the purpose of televising major championships and big tournaments. Sponsorship has helped in this and other areas of development, and with more and more companies in Europe becoming involved in the sport squash is ensured a bright future.

Although there is no real substitute for practice and application, books have an important role to play in helping you to improve your technique and

In 1986 Ross Norman became World Champion and, in so doing, ended the total supremacy of Jahangir Khan. His momentous victory was the culmination of intense physical and mental preparation

gain a deeper understanding of the game. This comprehensive guide, with clear instructional photographs and diagrams, provides all the information and advice you need to achieve better performances. The contributors make an impressive team and are internationally renowned for their knowledge and expertise. They have had a share in coaching me and other top squash players to success, and you, too, can benefit from their combined wisdom. *Improve Your Squash* is an authoritative manual to be recommended to all players of the game, to those who play for recreation as much as to those with serious competitive ambitions.

Ross Norman

Chapter 1 EQUIPMENT

Squash is a highly enjoyable and essentially uncomplicated game. The first step towards getting the most out of the sport is the right choice of equipment. This means not only using the correct racket and ball for your standard of play but also selecting the appropriate footwear and clothing to maxi- *mize safety, comfort and enjoyment. The basis of play at any level is how you grip the racket and where you carry it. Learn to build a winning game by getting to grips with the fundamentals of court coverage and recognizing the importance of the 'T' – the court's power position.*

The racket

It is unlikely that any game as simple and uncluttered as squash has received so much assistance from technological improvement.

Rackets are now produced in a wide range of materials, varying from the traditional laminated or cane wooden frame to injection-moulded plastics strengthened with space-age fibres. Prices have risen accordingly, of course, but there is little doubt that the new materials, many of them first utilized for ski design, have brought added dimensions of power and pace to the game.

There were suggestions in the early days of boron, kevlar, graphite, fibreglass and the rest of the innovative racket materials that a couple of years would see players returning to the tried and tested wooden models, clutching a variety of arm injuries and thirsting for their old sense of 'touch' and 'feel'. This has not happened. Even the most traditional of players finds it hard to resist the working quickness of the new light rackets, or the increased power and pace they bring to the drive, or the generally increased lifespan.

After early problems of brittle fragility and transferred vibration, which aggravated tennis elbow conditions for many players, the manufacturers of what have become generically known as graphite rackets are

Dimensions of a racket

(Appendix III of the ISRF rules of the international singles game of squash rackets)

1 Dimensions
Maximum length: 685mm/27in
Internal stringing
Maximum length: 215mm/8.5in
Maximum breadth: 184mm/7.25in
Framework of head
Maximum width across the face:
14mm/0.56in
Minimum width across the face:
9mm/0.36in
Maximum depth across the face:
20mm/0.81in
Minimum depth across the face:
12mm/0.47in
Shaft
Minimum thickness: 9mm/0.36in
Maximum weight (including stringing and bumper strip): 255g/9oz

2 Construction
At all times, the head or shaft shall not contain outside edges with a radius of curvature less than 2mm. String and string ends must be recessed within the racket head or, in cases where such recessing is impractical because of the racket material, or design, must be protected by a non-marking and securely attached bumper strip made of a flexible material which cannot crease into sharp edges following abrasive contact with floors or walls.

Strings shall be gut, nylon or a substitute material, providing metal is not used. Only two layers of string shall be allowed and these shall be alternately interlaced to form an orthogonal array.

Note to Referees on degradation
Rackets which have suffered damage so as to cause a potential hazard must not be used for play, unless the damaged region is repaired adhesively or by wound overlays, such that the damaged region becomes stronger than the material on either side of the damaged zone and has a smooth surface (G).

Manufacturers were given two years from 1 November, 1983, to allow rackets made of wood, but which do not meet the new specification, to clear the market. As from 1 November, 1985, *all* rackets must meet the above specification.

A selection of rackets and equipment showing the wide choice available to you when buying a squash kit

now producing wonderfully balanced, strong and vibration-damped models of virtually universal appeal.

Official standards of the International Squash Rackets Federation allow for almost any material in a racket, within specified dimension and safety limitations. Metal alloys have virtually replaced wood at the lower end of the price scale, but players of ambition have generally opted for graphite. (See also Chapter 6.)

Gripping the racket

There are absolute basics in every sport. In squash, the hard but simple game, there are just two: how to hold the racket and where to carry it. Later, it will become clear just how far skill and complexity can be developed upon such a narrow foundation.

The grip will be seen in many applications. Some prefer what is often termed the 'Pakistani' version, far up the handle with the guiding finger and thumb almost on the shaft. Others like a 'heel control', in which the butt of the handle fits to the base of the palm and the full length of the racket can be utilized in every shot. Such schools of thought are a matter of personal inclination. Practice will soon illustrate at which point an individual can best control the direction and the pace of the ball.

What is not open to debate, however, is the intrinsic shape of the grip, wherever it might be applied upon the handle of the racket. In squash

The racket designed for and by Ross Norman (right) and an injection-moulded racket designed to dissipate vibration (far right)

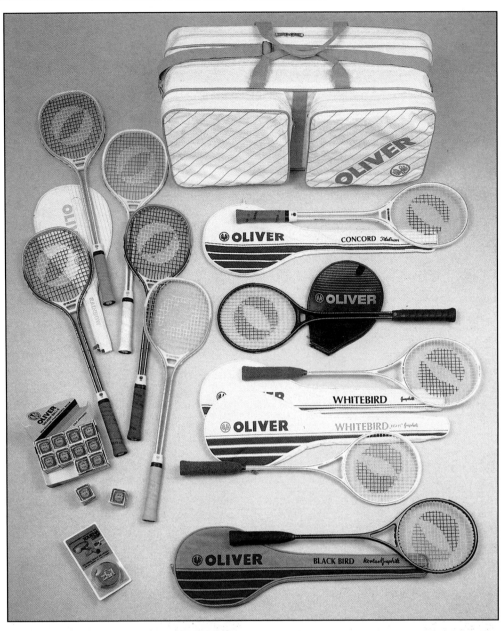

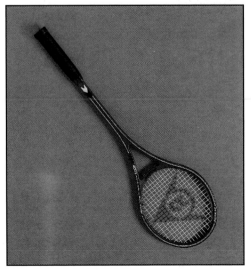

The racket

The grip is fundamental to good technique. Always remember the silent 'Shakehands' command and do not alter your grip during a rally

Support the racket head with your left hand and grasp the handle with your right, as if shaking hands with a friend

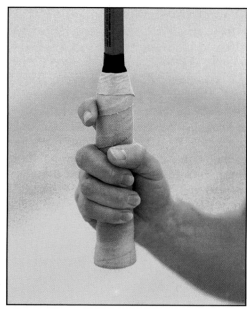

The player's view of the grip shows how the thumb and forefinger create a 'V' on the racket handle

The index finger curls around the top of the handle, and the other three fingers rest round the base, forming a firm holding vice

The grip seen from the underside: the thumb rests against the top edge of the second finger

there is not enough time for shifting and changing as in other games of greater leisure or larger environment. One grip is applied to a squash racket at the start of a rally and ideally should not alter until rest is again allowed. One respected coach pursued this philosophy to such a degree that he invented a special glove and handle cover made from Velcro interlocking material so that the racket was locked solid in the hand throughout the match.

Most complete players smile at such inflexibility today. There must, of course, be minute alterations and adjustments throughout a rally. Some players favour a shortening of the shaft for difficult straight drives from the deep back corners. Others like to loosen and lengthen their hold a little in the disguised boast. But superglue might not be too extreme an approach if it could condition all beginners to build their game upon the single correct grip before embarking on more advanced experimentation.

'Shakehands' is the silent command all squash players should direct at themselves when picking up their rackets. Holding the racket by the shaft in the non-playing hand and with the head at right angles to the floor, the handle should be approached with the playing hand precisely as though shaking hands with an old friend. The thumb and forefinger of the playing hand should form a 'V' shape on top of the handle, very slightly to the inner side so that the face of the racket is not even marginally open or closed in the ready position. The thumb and index finger effectively control the application of

the racket face; note that the index finger is curled around the top of the handle, and the other three fingers spread comfortably around the handle as the holding vice. The thumb rests against the top edge of the second finger.

The force of the grip should be sufficient to keep the racket firmly in the hand but relaxed enough to allow direction and control. Too tight a grip will soon generate tension in the forearm and often leads to tennis elbow, the dreaded affliction all racket players fear above everything else. Initially it is difficult to resist the urge to change grip during a rally, particularly when changing from one side to the other, but perseverance will be repaid in consistent control later.

It is worth the effort of shaking hands with your racket afresh at the start of every rally and, when court familiarity increases, making quick

The ideal ready position is on the 'T', the point from which every part of the court is most easily accessible, with the racket held up poised to play either a forehand or backhand

checks on the correct 'V' positioning when approaching a shot that allows time for such indulgence.

The companion command to 'Shakehands' is 'Cockwrist', because every shot in squash begins with the racket at ninety degrees to the arm in order to generate power through the wrist. Only shots that must be improvised under pressure should be played without cocking the wrist in advance.

Where to carry the racket
In the matter of where to carry this correctly held and readily cocked racket, the answer is, as ever, simple: to the centre of things.

The racket

Squash is played on a court 9.75m/ 32ft long and 6.40m/21ft wide. It has a 4.57m/15ft front wall and a 2.13m/7ft back wall. The tin is 0.48m/19in from the floor and the service cut line is 1.83m/6ft from the floor. Service boxes are 1.60m/5ft3in square. But the all-important measurement within that shape is the spot 3.20m/ 10ft6in from the side walls and 4.26m/13ft10in from the back wall where the centre line meets the short line to form the 'T'.

The 'T' is the fulcrum of a squash court; the point from which every part of the playing area is most easily accessible and on which a balanced posture gives the greatest likelihood of covering any shot an opponent can produce. Thus the ideal posture on a squash court is bouncing well balanced on the balls of the feet at the 'T', with the racket held in the cocked handshake manner, ready to move to either a forehand or backhand response.

More will be found in later pages on the essential footwork and movement that can bring simplest coverage of the entire court during play. Here it should be emphasized merely that, just as the best fitness and tactics cannot be applied without correct basic conditioned familiarity with the racket, the greatest speed and reaction in the world will not be enough if acceptance of the 'T' as central to all movement is not total.

Great and experienced players often shift their view of the 'T' to suit their own game plan or methodology. Some, like the tall and aggressive Stuart Davenport of New Zealand, advance further up the court the

Chris Robertson, in the ready position, bounces on the balls of his feet on the 'T'. Good position and balance are crucial to shot preparation

Court dimensions and nomenclature

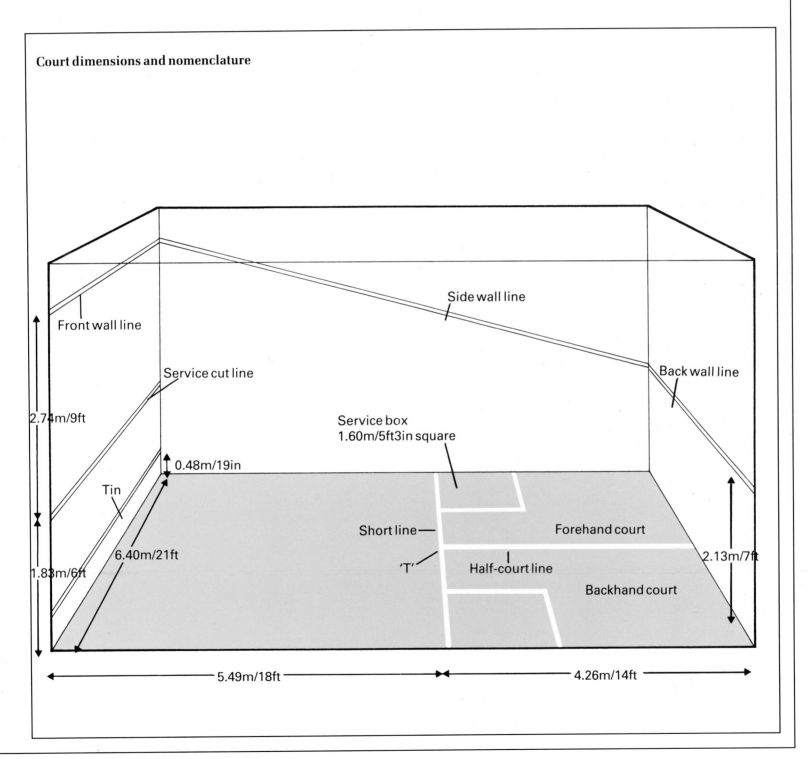

Front wall line

Side wall line

Service cut line

Back wall line

2.74m/9ft

Service box
1.60m/5ft3in square

0.48m/19in

Tin

Short line

Forehand court

'T'

Half-court line

2.13m/7ft

6.40m/21ft

1.83m/6ft

Backhand court

5.49m/18ft

4.26m/14ft

The racket

greater match pressure becomes, effectively shifting their personal 'T' towards the front wall. Others, like the amazingly fast Jansher Khan, are prepared to allow the game to drift backwards secure in the knowledge that they can reach the front of the court from a deliberately retarded 'T' quicker than almost anyone else. During his great undefeated five-and-a-half-year reign, the mighty Jahangir Khan habitually took the ball earlier, further up court, than anyone else, thus altering the entire geometry of the game for his opponents.

Although such players can and do change the placement of their personal 'T', none of them ever make the mistake of abandoning the basic creed of always developing their movement from that point.

Great changes have occurred in squash since the early days. Few clubs are without at least one glass-backed court these days. Some have three-sided glass courts around either a solid front wall or one solid side wall. There are demountable all-transparent showcourts of glass and Perspex which facilitate squash theatre-in-the-round for as many as 3,500 spectators at a time. Professionals lower tins to encourage more adventurous drop shots and remove cut lines to introduce attacking serves. But nobody ever suggested doing away with the 'T'.

Stuart Davenport plays from a personalized 'T' further up the court, towards the front wall. His height, aggressive play and confident position put his opponent, Jamie Hickox, under pressure

Squash theatre-in-the-round. Perspex courts allow large audiences to enjoy the spectacle. The increasing popularity of the sport is partly due to the improved TV coverage available with these courts

Demountable glass and Perspex courts have taken the game of squash out of the private clubs and into the public arena

Glass-backed squash courts are now to be found at most clubs. They allow a sizeable number of spectators to watch competitions

The ball

Balls of today would be virtually unrecognizable to the men who carried the game through its first century. Under the control of the International Squash Rackets Federation, companies like Dunlop and Merco now produce a range of squash balls for almost any circumstance to fine degrees of tolerance.

At club level particularly the player is well served. More so, in fact, than most club performers are prepared to acknowledge.

Because the top players of the game now play with a super-slow ball, known from its markings as the double dot yellow, many club players assume that they will be regarded as 'soft' if they are seen on court with anything less than the normally slow single yellow dot ball. In many cases, such as on cold courts or with a poor standard of opposition, they would be better off using one of the specially designed faster and springier balls designated in rising speed order as white dot, blue dot and red dot. Certainly young players or lightly muscled women enjoy a far more rounded and rewarding game when they use a ball more suited to their weight of shot and running speed.

Even top professionals will train with a white spot if the courts are cold or if they want to simulate the power and pace of a respected future opponent. Greater usage should be made throughout the game of this unique facility of altering the speed of the ball to suit conditions or requirements.

Certainly the professional game has carried the theory to far limits in the other direction. Not only has the super-slow double dot been adopted for all major competition play throughout the world, to compensate for improving fitness and technique throughout the game at that level, but special reflective balls and white balls have been developed for play under television cameras and on the coloured floors of the all-transparent showcourts.

Specifications of a squash racket ball

(Appendix IV of the ISRF rules of the international singles game of squash rackets)

The following ball specification is for the standard ISRF championship yellow dot ball:

Mass (weight): 23.2 – 24.6g
Diameter: 39.5 – 41.5mm

1 Rebound

The rebound test is performed on balls stabilized at 20°C using a sealed concrete floor surface. The percentage rebound is measured from the bottom of the ball. Specification measurement 16 – 17%.

2 Deflection

The deflection is measured as the meniscus (ink spot diam) diameter shown when the ball is compressed under a load of 5.2kg between two glass plates.
Specification measurement 27.18 – 30.48mm/1.07 – 1.2in.

3 Seam strength

Required seam length for strength test is 2.54cm/1in.
Seam strength is the load required to separate a 2.54cm length of seam. The load is applied normal to the seam and measured on a Scott Tensile Tester.
The load is gradually increased until the seam separates and the maximum load is recorded.
The minimum seam strength specification is 10.5kg/cm (60lb/in). The average test result is 13.4kg/cm (75lb/in).

The 'teleball', developed for use under television cameras. Reflective inserts highlight the ball, causing it to glow clearly on a television screen

It is important always to watch the ball, especially when you are preparing to strike it. Top players like Ross Norman seldom make the mistake of taking their eye off the ball

When choosing the type of ball to use, you should take into account your standard of play, level of fitness, running speed and weight of shot as well as the condition of the court

Clothing

Shoes are the clothing item requiring most attention from the squash player. Two hours and more on court at a time, at constant running speed, with much twisting and turning, several times a week, places tremendous stress upon the feet.

Luckily, squash shoe manufacturers have responded to the need. Most quality shoes now feature lightness of weight, strength of supports, sureness of grip and adequate ventilation.

Some physiotherapists are concerned that too many designs still incorporate high heel support, which they believe is damaging to the Achilles tendon. There is one well-known squash physio who begins all consultations by putting a blade through the heel tab of her patients' squash shoes.

Preferences vary, of course, on particular models and designs, but the serious squash player should be looking for firm, all-round support of the foot without undue pressure in any area. Blisters are a problem with all players and it is important to remember that poor upper fitting can produce just as much discomfort and pain from blisters on the toes or insteps as poor soles can beneath.

Two pairs of socks can reduce the friction between shoe and foot, but remember to buy shoes that will accommodate comfortably the extra thickness. Sometimes careful selection of good quality socks is every bit as important as the shoes placed around them.

The greatest advance in the foot department for all athletes, but particularly squash players whose weight descends upon the heel and ball of the foot so hard and so often, is the new generation of shock-absorbing inners. These have been developed from materials originally designed in imitation of human tissue to protect the delicate instrumentation of space craft. Available as either full insoles or pads for heel or ball, these materials reduce bruising and shock soreness dramatically.

Clothing can be of any pastel shade that will contrast with the black balls now generally in use. At professional level reverse applications are now in use, with darker clothing being worn to contrast with the white balls used

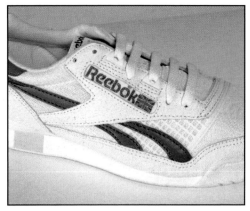

There are many types of squash shoe on the market. Make sure you buy ones that give you maximum strength, support and flexibility

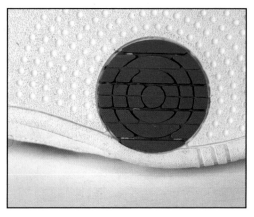

Constant twisting and turning of the body and repeated running back and forth across the court demand shoes that have a sureness of grip

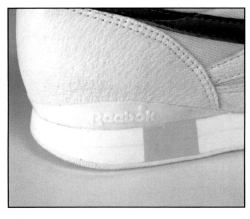

Soles need to be thick enough to absorb the shock of constantly shifting your weight from the balls of the feet to the heels

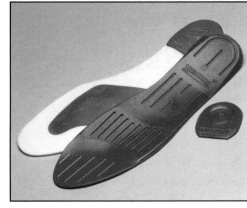

The new generation of shock-absorbing inners can help reduce the risk of bruising and shock soreness to the feet and lower legs

Susan Devoy in a cotton warmer top ideal for knocking up prior to matchplay and cooling down after it

Jahangir Khan in a shell suit of man-made fibre, usually worn over cotton warmers outside the court

on coloured floors and gray-hued glass or plastic courts.

Most squash is still played against white plaster walls, however, and light colours work best. Comfort and lack of abrasion are the main points to strive for and, generally, cotton provides the best option in play. Most men are content to play in cotton T-shirts these days. Shorts vary from football style to the very brief athletic style. Women usually train in the same apparel but still tend to prefer a skirted outfit for matchplay.

Perhaps the most ignored element of squash dress is the warming up and warming down accoutrement. The stretching, twisting and sprinting that is instantly required in squash from the first rally means that careful warming up is essential and maintenance of that condition from dressing-room to court equally vital. Similarly, standing around draughty courts and corridors after two hours of extreme exercise demands some protective attitudes.

Most regular players these days wear three layers of clothing through their warm-up, competition and warm-down period. Playing kit is covered by a light cotton warmer suit, which is in turn covered by a shell suit of man-made fibre such as the Tactel now produced by ICI and much in use by athletes of all kinds. (See also Chapter 6.)

Match report STRENGTH AND STAMINA

Event: Patrick International Festival
Venue: Chichester, UK
Date: 30 March, 1983
Scoreline: Jahangir Khan (Pakistan)
bt Gamal Awad (Egypt)
9–10 9–5 9–7 9–2

Jahangir Khan had been unbeaten for almost two years when he took on Gamal Awad in the 1983 final of the Chichester Festival. During that time a number of theories had been put forward on how to defeat the seemingly invincible young man from Peshawar. But no one had come close to putting these into successful practice.

Gamal Awad felt that opponents often gave up too soon against Jahangir Khan. The Pakistani's stamina needed to be tested to the full, Awad felt, and to that end he went to Jonah Barrington, who pushed him through a rigorous training programme designed to improve his fitness. Barrington had turned himself into the best player in the world some years earlier by honing his body to the peak of physical perfection. The Egyptian hoped that a similarly punishing regime allied to his already remarkable retrieving ability would permit him to lengthen the rallies sufficiently to bring about the downfall of Jahangir Khan.

'I have only been able to complete half the course,' Awad admitted at Chichester. 'But it has certainly helped my confidence.' There was nothing wrong with the plan in essence. And for periods of the match it worked perfectly. Eventually, however, it simply paid tribute to Jahangir Khan's own superior fitness, which he acknowledged was tested to the full for the first time since he had begun his run back in 1981. Sadly, it

Jahangir Khan (left) obviously working harder than Gamal Awad, but eventually a winner through superior strength and stamina

also ended the challenge of Awad for the world crown. Next time out against Jahangir Khan he managed just one point and was never again capable of seriously threatening the very best in the game.

Let us get back to Chichester. Awad detained the world champion for two hours and 45 minutes, beating the previous longest recorded match by some ten minutes. Along the way, the two demolished every other record in the book by taking one hour 11 minutes for the opening game, one hour 49 minutes for the first two, and two hours 31 minutes to complete three – all new barriers for which those fit enough are still aiming. Awad was eventually vanquished, but not be-

fore he had contributed fully to one of the most talked about matches in the annals of squash.

Eight minutes went by before Jahangir Khan registered the first point of the match. He moved to 2–0 after ten minutes and another three had slipped by before Awad found a back wall nick with a service to open his account. It was still 2–1 after 23 minutes but then, despite some magnificent full-length retrieving by the former soccer goalkeeper, Jahangir Khan began to edge ahead.

The Pakistani moved to 8–1 after 38 minutes and the 1,200 spectators awaited the inevitable kill. It was not to come and Awad took his second point of the match three minutes later

A world duration record of 2hrs 45mins. Gamal looks the cooler but Jahangir was the fitter, a master of concentrated effort

to begin a fight-back never to be forgotten by those present in the Chichester Theatre. The ball burst after 48 minutes of the first game, by which time the little Egyptian had pulled back to 5–8 with a backhand drive, a nick boast and a tinned drop from Jahangir Khan.

More mistakes followed from the world champion; he was penalized a point when a loose shot came back to him in mid-court and two hurried strokes found the tin to take the score to 8–8. A forehand drive gave him his second game-ball at 9–8 but Awad regained service and levelled the score again with a perfect length lob.

The subsequent rally lasted eight minutes and included nearly 300 strokes. It ended in a let. The next exchange consisted of just nine strokes before Jahangir Khan found the tin with a forehand boast. So the first game went to Awad after 71 minutes and his game plan seemed to be coming together.

That feeling persisted at the beginning of the second game as Jahangir Khan made two unforced errors and conceded a stroke to let Awad away to a 3–1 lead. Then Jahangir Khan's famous backhand drop began to find the target and, with the help of a penalty stroke, he eased to 5–3.

Awad chose this point to retreat once more into a defensive shell. Nine of the ensuing eleven rallies ended in lets and over a 17-minute period only two points were scored. They were both credited to Awad but he threw away his hard-earned advantage by clattering the tin with two attempted winners in quick succession. Jahangir Khan led 7–5; pre-

cisely one hour and 40 minutes had elapsed. Awad did regain service but Jahangir Khan won it back after a three-minute rally and moved to game-ball by ending a five-minute skirmish with a splendid forehand cross-court winner. Awad lost out in an exchange of drops and the game was Jahangir Khan's, 9–5 in 38 minutes.

It seemed certain that one player would soon crack. Incredibly, however, the third game lasted 41 minutes. Jahangir Khan found the tin three times to present Awad once again with the early lead. Awad proved equally generous over the next few rallies and Jahangir Khan levelled the score at 3–3.

The activity, it seemed, was proving more strenuous for the balls than the players; the second gave up the ghost after two hours of the match. By the time a replacement had been warmed up, however, the two gladiators eventually and understandably began to show real signs of strain. Lets and mistakes became the order of the day as the score seesawed to 6–6. A stroke took Jahangir Khan to 7–6, and a winning drop gave him game-ball. He had to wait a further ten minutes, though, to press home the advantage and move into a 2–1 lead.

It was inevitable that the loser of that third game would fall away from the pace. Jahangir Khan quickly moved to 6–0 and only one point was secured by a winner; two came from penalty strokes and three from Awad errors. But Jahangir Khan was tired, too. He dropped a backhand into the tin and later, when Awad returned the compliment to give the Pakistani match-ball, crashed what should have been the title-winning drive into the same vicinity. He repeated the mistake in the next rally but then regained the service and appropriately closed out Awad's colossal challenge with his favourite backhand drop.

Awad had set out to lengthen the rallies, to use his tremendous retrieving and newly-honed fitness to drag the world champion into a prolonged and painful battle. He did just that but it was his opponent who emerged as the superior physical specimen.

Jahangir Khan's stamina would never again be questioned. He went from strength to strength to establish a remarkable unbeaten run stretching over five and a half years. Gamal Awad had given his all but sadly it had taken a deadly toll. The little Egyptian, known throughout the squash world as 'Grasshopper', was destined never to regain his bounce.

Chapter 2 THE STROKES

Squash is a deceptively simple game; its finesse lies in masterly strokeplay, being selective and using discretion. It has as much to do with judgment, knowing when to play which shot from where, as it has to do with execution, being able to hit the ball with precision and the appropriate power. This chapter examines the fundamental moves and shows you how to develop them into the full range of squash strokes, including the serve which acts as an initiator of strategy, forcing your opponent to play as you want and not vice versa. Once you have built a solid and confident game, you are ready to exploit your opponent's weaknesses and produce punishing winning shots.

Playing requirements

Leaving the mind aside for now, the principal requirements to play the game of squash are the ability to move and the ability to use the racket. Fortunately for many of us neither ability is needed in abundance to enjoy a modest game of squash. For one of the several important advantages squash enjoys is that you do not have to be particularly proficient to play to a standard that will afford pleasure and exercise. An ordinary tennis player, for example, will almost certainly have problems serving and, even if that crucial skill is reasonably mastered, the net still has to be crossed with every shot he makes. Much of the time will be spent picking up and retrieving balls, none of which is designed to give the desirable exercise. Providing the squash player finds partners of a fairly similar standard, and has a reasonable ability to move and use a racket, he will be on his way.

What progress is made will then relate to athleticism and racket skills, the development of which will greatly depend on the player's inclinations. For progress inevitably goes hand in hand with diligence and persistence. Top-class performers in any sport make little reference to talent, but they are quick to stress the need for application. Rarely do squash players possess the balanced blend of physical attributes and ball skills that would be most desirable. For this reason, you see players who can run fast and for a long time, but have little idea what to do with the ball. Conversely, you see players who can hardly move but who have considerable natural skill with the racket.

At all levels, from veterans to juniors, a balanced blend of fitness, agility and racket skill is required

Progress can definitely be made by the runner – indeed, there are several examples of players at the top of the sport internationally and certainly at the top in the UK whose main ability

Zarak Jahan, 1988 British Open Under-23 Champion, displays the extraordinary flexibility of his younger limbs to reach an angled drop shot from Nigel Stiles

is to hunt the ball relentlessly – and you will be able to hold your own if you can use the racket skilfully. However, if you have an obvious deficiency in either category, any opponent with his wits about him will be quick to exploit your weaknesses, which are usually not hard to spot.

If you are physically unfit or not strong enough, balanced regular training, which does not have to be time-consuming, should quickly help to put that right. More difficult might be improving your racket skills, if by nature they do not come too easily. However, even the best players have to practise regularly, so hitting the squash ball as often as possible will undoubtedly help, especially if you have had some guidance on the technical requirements of the strokes. Since squash is a technical game, there would be only limited profit in hitting the ball repeatedly in an incorrect fashion.

All ball sports require their participants to move as well as possible and squash, since it is such a taxing game physically, makes greater demands than most. Racket players of such games as squash, tennis and badminton may often be different sporting animals from rugby and soccer players, who are used to a bigger ball and no racket. Cricketers and hockey players are often capable squash players, as they belong to the small-ball category, and tennis and badminton usually convert to squash quite readily. Many squash clubs are, of course, attached to tennis clubs and although both games tend now to be played all year round, tennis and squash still complement each other seasonally.

Perhaps oddly, and it may only be coincidental, there are several players who have taken up squash successfully after rugby careers. Many of them have been quite skilful, not having to rely on their formidable physiques, which might be just as well!

Clubs

It is not difficult these days to start playing squash. In the UK, there is no longer the shortage of facilities that existed in the pre-Barrington era, when squash courts were the province of public schools, officers' messes and private clubs.

Commercial clubs and public leisure centres have been added to the private clubs, so nobody is likely to find they have nowhere to play. The clubs will provide social benefits, generally not available in leisure centres, and will probably help you to find your level and suitable opponents more readily.

There may be many reasons for wanting to play squash: you may simply want to take more exercise, in which case squash has advantages over running as it takes place indoors and is safe from the vagaries of the weather; for the businessman, squash may bring relief from tension in the satisfying striking of the ball against the wall; others may be trying to become capable squash players. These reasons are all valid and there is room in any well-run club for players of all types and all standards.

Having said that it is a relatively simple matter to play to a modest standard, it should not be assumed that the game is simple. A look at the court itself also tends to lend support to the same assumption. But even for those who have been in the game a long time, there is always something new to learn. Indeed, although young players do reach high standards at an early age, there are many players who mature later, as if they needed time to learn the game's secrets.

When the legs are less willing than of yore, craft and subtlety, the hallmarks of thinking old age, take over. It is far from unusual to see younger, fitter and very willing players outmanoeuvred and eventually outplayed by wilier, senior players. For which we should, as we grow older, all be extremely grateful. The veteran (over forty-five) and vintage (over fifty-five) categories are very popular and, for the inexperienced, time spent watching the best in those groups is time well-spent.

Hitting the ball straight

The first thing to do, once on court, is to learn to hit the ball correctly, since a sound, dependable swing is the foundation of everything you will subsequently want to do with the racket. Some players will have a natural swing, just as in golf, but more will not and these will need to understand the mechanics of the swing, without becoming technically obsessed by them.

When things are going wrong, even the world's best golfers pay attention to the swing and, whilst it may not be so critical for them, squash players out of form could do a lot worse than examine their swing, or better still have someone examine it for them. It is a simple matter for faults to creep into the swing under the pressure of matchplay and, if these faults are not quickly corrected, they can create major problems, as they become more and more entrenched.

Important to the swing is a high, though not wide, and early preparation of the racket: if the racket is taken well back, there will be a fullness of stroke, which will assist in controlling the ball, besides adding to the power. Smoothness and rhythm are crucial to the swing from the highest point of the preparation to the full extent of the follow-through. Any rushing or loss of composure will inevitably cause snatching and deviation of the racket head, which will lead to error.

A smooth, controlled swing is part of the relaxation that is most necessary in the game of squash. The idea that the game is about dashing around and expending as much energy as possible is sadly mistaken. Apart from leaving you in a state of exhaustion, probably quite early in the game, it will hardly allow you to produce the racket correctly and put the ball into areas of the court that are disadvantageous to your opponents. The lack of composure brought about by rushing inevitably leads to muddled thought processes and, no matter how fit and strong you may be, it is still in

Forehand swing

1 A high backswing with the racket overhead and a bent arm shows good preparation. Concentrating on the ball, the player is about to move her weight on to the front foot.

2 The racket moves back and down, with the elbow and butt of the racket handle being pulled through. The player is now in a strong stance, giving stability to the stroke.

3 Just before impact the forearm is about to turn through the impact point. This turning of the arm is called pronation.

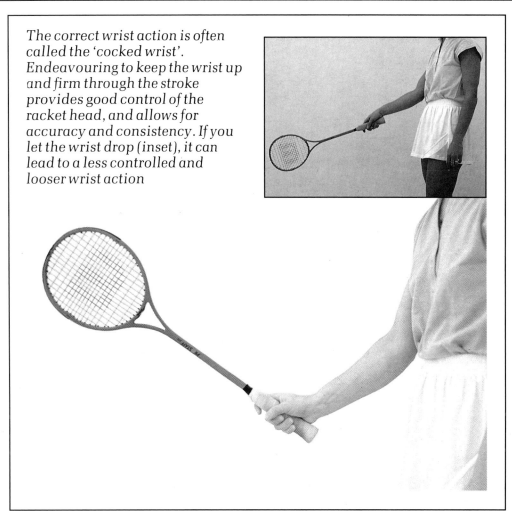

your interests to use your brain.

Maintaining composure applies to any sport you can think of, so it is sound advice to take your time if things are going badly. Natural anxiety makes anyone hurry in such circumstances, so it demands a concentrated mental effort to keep control.

Also important in the basic swing is the need to keep the wrist up and firm. Holding it up means that the racket head will also be high and the firmness means that deviations of the racket head will be kept to a minimum. It is easy to prove to yourself how important the wrist is: take hold of the racket, then turn the wrist this way and that and you will easily see

4 At impact, the player is well-balanced, has total concentration on the ball and good control over the racket head with the correct grip and a firm wrist.

5 The swing has come across the player's body in a relaxed action without excessive twisting. It hinges on the elbow and the wrist is still up, keeping control of the racket head.

6 The racket has swung through to a full follow-through position, indicating a powerful stroke. The swing has moved from a 'V' in the backswing to a 'V' in the follow-through.

THE STROKES

Backhand swing

1 The racket is held high overhead, with the shoulder relaxed and turned and the elbow back and across the body. Again, note the cocked wrist and 'V' shape.

2 The player's weight moves forward as the racket moves down and around the body on its path to impact point.

3 The elbow and butt of the racket are pulled through, and the forearm is about to turn, generating racket-head speed through impact point. This is called supination.

Forehand drive

1 From a ready position the player, concentrating on the ball, starts to move off and is already preparing the racket on his forehand side.

2 For a forehand straight drive, the player moves to a position at the side of the ball, facing the side wall. He has turned his body and prepared his racket.

3 The player waits for the ball to come back between him and the side wall. At this point he is correctly positioned to drive the ball straight.

4 Note how the arm has straightened out at impact, the body is well-balanced and the player has total concentration on the ball.

5 The swing flows through across the body, turning at the elbow and shoulder. Note how the wrist is still up, providing good control of the racket head for a grooved swing.

6 The full follow-through. Note how the body is still balanced and the racket has travelled through smoothly and without interruption in a large curve, generating power and control.

4 As he prepares to swing, the player's weight moves forward into the shot and he endeavours to stay steady and balanced while swinging.

5 Just before impact, as the elbow and racket butt are pulled through and the racket is about to accelerate to impact point, the player shows total concentration and perfect poise.

6 The body has turned through the shot but still shows good balance, and the racket good control in the full follow-through position. The player is still focusing on the impact point.

Hitting the ball straight

the effect the various movements of the wrist have on the racket head.

Any time spent in developing a controlled, relaxed swing is time well-spent; although it is clear that beginners will need to give the swing extra attention, it is worth bearing in mind its importance even when you have reached a worthwhile standard.

Initially when you go on court with a partner, you will be engaged in hitting the ball backwards and forwards to each other, cross-court and in a co-operative rather than a competitive manner. This will be the time, therefore, to concentrate on swinging properly. Soon, however, especially as you move into competitive situations, it will be necessary to learn to hit the ball straight; this does not mean, however, that cross-court hitting is unimportant.

Hitting the ball straight (the straight drive) means striking the ball so that it goes directly from the front wall to the back wall, without hitting the side wall. It is also crucially important that the straight hit is struck as close to the side wall as possible. This has the advantage of keeping the ball away from the centre of the court, always to be recommended since that is a position any opponent will be keen to adopt. It also creates difficulty for your opponent, since no player, regardless of his level of play, finds it easy to play the ball satisfactorily when it is close to the wall.

Should the straight hit make contact with the side wall, it can easily be seen that it will come out towards the centre of the court. Contact with the side wall also has the disadvantage of slowing down the passage of the ball, thus giving your opponent more time to retrieve it.

Hitting the ball straight may sound and even look simple enough, but it is anything but that. It requires constant practice, even after the shot is to some extent mastered.

Affecting the direction of the shot is the control of the racket head through the ball and perhaps first of all the position adopted to make the shot. If you get too close to the ball, there is little chance of hitting it straight; if

Backhand drive

1 The player moves off for the backhand drive, concentrating on the ball and preparing the racket as soon as possible.

2 For a straight drive, he will move up or down the court to a position to the side of the ball.

3 The player turns his body to face the side wall, the position used for straight shots. He has turned his shoulder and started to take his racket to a backswing position.

the balance is wrong, the ball may go anywhere; if you move as you strike the ball, it is unlikely that you will be able to keep it straight.

Although under pressure they may not always be easily obtainable, the best positions to hit straight from the front of the court are when you lead off the front foot. These positions will give a forward inclination of the body, maintain the movement of the racket and body in the same direction, keep the head over the ball and generally establish a balanced position from which to strike the ball.

As you move further back in the court it will prove more difficult to set up a front foot position, but this should not stop you trying if you have

sufficient time. For the principles of balance and harmony remain, wherever you are in the court, however much pressure you are under.

Closeness to the wall is a prime factor and, if that can be achieved, it really will not matter at what pace and height the ball is struck. High on the front wall and without pace is perfectly effective if it is close to the wall, but once the shot strays, it will be very vulnerable to attack, especially to those players with the ability to hit the ball off the volley into the cross-court nick.

However, the main consideration when hitting straight is to strike the ball harder; and, particularly if you wish to exert pressure on an oppo-

nent, to hit it low. Even if the ball th strays from the side wall it will ha the advantage of being low and the fore more difficult to pick up. A lo struck ball also spends less time the air, so giving the opponent le time to get into position.

The straight hit will provide a pla form from which to play. When play ed well it will cause an opponent t make loose returns that you ca attack. The inability to play straigh accurately will cause acute problem: and so consolidation of the technique should be a central part of any play er's practice. If you do not practise regularly then you should at least be aware when playing games of how important the shot is.

4 The player, perfectly poised, shows good balance and racket preparation, while waiting for the ball to fall down between him and the side wall to the desired impact point.

5 When the ball reaches the ideal position for the shot, the player starts to swing while focusing on the ball. He is still well-balanced with knees bent and weight forward.

6 At the end of the shot the player's body is still facing the side wall, showing that he has been correctly positioned for a straight drive.

Cross-court hitting

Hitting the ball cross-court is of similar significance to hitting the ball straight; indeed, when played badly it will transfer initiative in a rally almost more than any other stroke.

Often the striker will be in the front areas of the court in control of the rally. Although the cross-court hit may not be the most desirable of the options available and is played far too frequently, it will do little harm if it is played accurately. Played inaccurately, that is through the middle of the court or short, hitting the side wall too early and therefore leaving the ball in the middle of the court, and your centrally-placed opponent will be in an ideal position to capitalize on the mistake and either finish the rally or at least put you under extreme pressure.

The secret of the well-played cross-court hit is to find the correct width, at the same time keeping the ball low. Since, even if the ball is hit on the correct line, but is relatively high in the air, it will be vulnerable to interception by the alert volleyer.

If the opponent is in the orthodox central position in the court, it is important to have a clear picture of where you need to strike the ball. The ideal width, which should pass even the most agile of players, should be aimed on a line that would take the ball to the side wall about 30–45cm/ 12–18in to the back of the service box. There are, in fact, no great margins of error. Stray from that line at your peril.

If you want proof of the importance of cross-court play, watch any match with this in mind and you will easily see how it affects the outcome of any

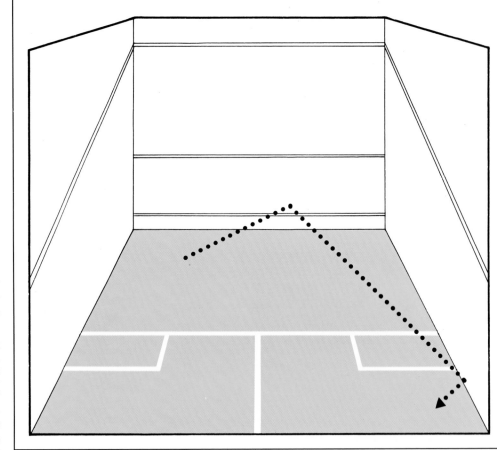

The cross-court hit should be played with the correct width, keeping the ball low. The ideal line would take the ball to the side wall about 30–45cm/12–18in behind the service box

encounter. At the top levels of the game, the Pakistanis seem to play cross-court with more awareness than anybody. That may be because they believe in cross-court play and have therefore perfected it.

If you master the straight and the cross-court hits you will be well on your way to providing yourself with a basis from which to play. Equally, until you achieve some sort of mastery of these shots, you will be at a serious disadvantage. Do not be deceived by the apparent simplicity of the task, however; it is not easy even for players of a high standard.

Volleying

Volleying is by no means an easy proposition, but to move into a game situation it is a shot that you will soon need as part of your repertoire. To begin a game satisfactorily you will be required to serve, which involves hitting the ball out of the hand before it bounces, a form of volley that requires similar timing. To deal with your opponent's serve you will often be called on to volley, since that is how the ball reaches you.

Therefore, although it is a difficult proposition you cannot ignore the volley, even in the early stages. Certainly, it will quickly show up any

problems with control of the racket. There is little scope for any deviations of the racket face and positioning; as with all shots in squash, they are of paramount importance. It is a common fault to get too near the ball when volleying and this causes all manner of complications. The volley is always best played when you are comfortably stretched into the ball.

The volley may reach you at varying heights, but most commonly

Phil Kenyon shapes to volley overhead, deep on the forehand, taking time from his opponent and turning defence into attack

Overhead volley

1 Reaching up for an overhead volley, the player demonstrates classic preparation for the smash action.

2 This shot is similar to the tennis serve. The overarm throwing action replaces the side-arm action of drives.

3 On this attacking volley, the swing comes up and over the ball and diagonally down across the body.

Volleying

at shoulder height, and each shot will require adjustments of technique. The overhead volley, for instance, is more akin to the tennis smash and will require a sense of timing that brings the racket smoothly through the ball, even though it will often be an attacking stroke. Any quickening of the rhythm will inevitably lead to the ball ending up in the tin or even the floor.

Played well, aimed at the nick, the overhead volley can be highly satisfying, both in contact off the racket and where the ball finishes.

The volley that reaches you at shoulder height will be generally comfortable to play, not least because of the number of times you are required to play it. When well practised it should not create undue difficulty, and it should eventually be a matter of the range of shots you are able to produce from it.

Once the ball begins to drop from its highest point, it will become increasingly difficult to hit a volley. Volleys that are dropping are not at all easy, especially for tall players, who must always remember the need to

get down for the low volley. Failure to do that will lead to error.

Another volley that causes problems is the one struck straight at you, often made worse if it is low as well. What is needed to combat the volley, aimed at you intentionally or otherwise, is quick use of the racket, allied to early preparation. If the racket is up and ready, you will have a better chance of making contact than if it is down by your ankles. Where possible it is also advisable to bend the body in an effort to make room for the racket. You will not always have time to

Adjusting to volley aimed at body

1 The player has moved well into the front court, following up on a short ball and looking for a volley to intercept. He has the racket raised preparing for a reflex volley and is on his toes for a quick reaction.

2 A fast loose ball has come directly at the player, who has quickly created room and turned to allow a side-on stroke.

3 This rapid exchange of shots has allowed no time for classic stroke-play, but a fast, punching volley will put considerable pressure on his opponent.

Low volley

move the feet, but if you remain in a solid, upright position you are less likely to be able to manoeuvre the racket successfully.

Volleys can, of course, be played at any pace, but the essential requirement of racket-head control through the ball will be the same whatever type of volley is attempted.

Volleying will help you to return the serve and thus engage in a rally, and as you improve it will increasingly become a means of attack, enabling you to cut off the ball before it reaches the troublesome deep areas of the court. By cutting the ball off, you will also be allowing your opponent less time to recover or to take up suitable, balanced positions.

By operating across the mid-court line, which is not too taxing on the movement, you may, if your volleying is of sufficient quality, be able to maintain pressure on your opponent. If you are in the habit of letting the ball pass you on the volley, apart from missing a chance to attack, you are allowing your opponent more time and may be creating more difficult shots for yourself.

Volleying at all costs is not the answer, but discriminate, selective volleying will always pay dividends when well executed.

1 Early preparation is crucial to create time for the swing on the volley. Here the player moves forward with good preparation while concentrating intently on the ball.

2 Bracing himself in a strong stance and twisting his upper body to create power in the swing, the player prepares to strike.

3 On the follow-through, the player demonstrates that he has been able to maintain good balance throughout the shot, although playing a fairly difficult ball.

Angles

The angle, which is any shot that hits the side wall before reaching the front wall (in some circumstances also known as the boast), is a shot of some consequence. There are not too many players who are adept at playing angles and, when played badly, they are very vulnerable.

The first and most important angle is the one played from deep in the court. This is necessary to survive if the service has prevented you from volleying and so found its way into the back corners. Just as the volley is needed to return the service, the angle is required to give you other options, especially if you are confronted by consistently accurate serving. The angle is, in fact, the last line of defence, when you have failed to inter-

cept the service or failed to play the ball straight or cross-court after it has bounced. The server will be quite happy to see you forced into playing an angle, since it is easily observable and gives him plenty of time to take up position at the front of the court. It therefore becomes of crucial importance to play the shot as well as possible, which is low over the tin and wide, if possible looking for the nick close to the front wall. Some high-standard players, indeed, become very skilled at playing the angle for the nick. When successful, they have transformed what is primarily a defensive situation into one where they win the point outright. But that will not be everybody's lot and most players will have to settle for playing it as

well as possible.

As with most shots in squash, what will help you to play angles well is correct positioning and this applies particularly to those played from deep in the court. There are several positional faults that may occur. First, there is a tendency to follow the ball into the corners, thus leaving little room for the swing and generally getting too close to the ball. This will cause errors. It is therefore important to keep well away from the ball and the side wall to make sure you can swing fully through the ball. Angles must be struck firmly, otherwise they will not have sufficient impetus to carry to the front wall.

Often players will be seen pulling away from the shot, another failing

Forehand boast

1 From the position for receiving service, the player has a number of options. From a good serve, you will sometimes be forced to boast, but try to avoid this if possible.

2 The player prepares to move, while assessing the serve to see which shot she will have to play and from which position.

3 For a boast she will turn to face the back corner and position herself to the side of the ball.

Australia's Kelvin Smith leads off the front foot as he prepares to play a forehand boast

again caused by being too near the wall or by being too eager to move back to a central position. Desirable though it may be to recover a central position, it should not be at the cost of playing a weak shot or even failing to get the ball up.

Wherever possible it is best to lead into the angle off the front foot – left on the forehand, right on the backhand – since this maintains the right balance as well as helping to get the body into the shot, which will help to provide the necessary power.

Other problems with the shot may be related to the racket head and the most common fault is to close the racket face on the forehand side. The results are obvious: the ball ends up in the tin.

4 It is important to get under the ball when boasting from the back of the court. Note how the racket is well prepared and the player is starting to bend her knees.

5 Here the racket is about to come under the ball and lift it on to the side wall.

6 From a low angle, we see the ball on its way to the front after rebounding off the side. The swing has come from under the ball into a compact and controlled follow-through.

Angles

When the position adopted is not sufficiently sideways-on to the side wall, there is a tendency to hit the ball too far ahead of your feet, thus producing an inaccurate shot which will not make a wide enough angle and, more often than not, will end up in the centre of the court. If the angle is not struck far enough in front of the feet (i.e. too directly at the side wall) it will fail to reach the front wall.

All of this is about the forehand deep angle and it is true to say that the backhand angle affords fewer problems, which is also the case with technique generally on the backhand side.

The beginner may initially have more difficulty in hitting the backhand, but once his standard improves, he will very often find it technically easier and will invariably have a greater range of shots down the backhand side. For instance, the ball knocked in short from three-quarter-court is commonly played on the backhand and usually quite well. There are few players who can play the same shot on the forehand side.

The backhand deep angle involves the same technical considerations as the forehand: front-foot lead, keeping away from the ball and the side wall; not going too far into the corner and making sure you maintain control of the racket head. Generally, the preparation of the racket is better on the backhand than on the forehand and that helps to produce a better angle.

The deep, defensive angle is the most important of the angles, but those played at the front, the short angles, have their own value. These are attacking shots used as a variation at the front of the court. They will be particularly effective when employed in harness with the straight drop. If you play the drop bringing your opponent into the front corners, when he is sufficiently lulled into looking for the shot, the insertion of the short angle should, if played well, leave your opponent in no-man's-land. It will obviously be best if played with a little delay and it should not be played too often. Once it is looked for, it will not be as effective. If you have the shot under control, it can

Backhand boast

1 The player prepares to boast from mid-court. This is often an attacking boast, used to move an opponent from the back to the front of the court.

2 The player has prepared his racket, positioned himself to the side of the ball and turned slightly more to the back than he would for a straight drive.

3 It is important when boasting to create room for the shot and not cramp up the stroke. Here the player waits for the ball to come into the best position for a boast.

win you a crucial point and should ideally have an element of surprise about it, but it is not an easy shot to play and requires considerable racket control. Positioning, although it may not be of an orthodox nature, remains important, since closeness to the ball, over-running of the ball and closeness to the wall may all lead to error. It is a shot that may be played from improvised positions, provided that the feet are still, but if a front-foot position can be achieved it will have the added advantage of helping to disguise the intention.

As with the deeper angle, the forehand short angle is a more difficult proposition technically, largely for the same reasons, i.e. the positioning is less likely to be right. Some players become adept at the shot, though not too many, but whatever its difficulties, its possibilities should not be overlooked.

The reverse angle has similar advantages to the short angle insofar as it is played with the intention to surprise. The reverse angle is played across the body to hit the side wall furthest away from the prepared racket first. It can be played from positions at the front and back of the court, but the danger that exists when playing from the front is that it may come back towards you. Played from the back, especially against opponents who are not careful watchers, the shot can be very deceptive. As with all angles, the reverse angle is best played as low to the tin as possible. This gives opponents less to play off.

Mostly, angles will be well struck. If indeed they are played with insufficient purpose, half-heartedly, there is every chance that the ball will not

4 The desired impact point is when the ball has passed the player. It is here that the correct angle into the side wall can be gained.

5 Use a compact swing when boasting as this will give both control and touch to the shot.

6 Good balance and racket control at the end of the shot. The ball has been allowed to pass the player, has been stroked into the side wall and is rebounding towards the front wall.

Short angle

1 This player uses the same preparation for the short angle as for the backhand straight drive. This helps disguise the shot.

2 The player moves to the side of the ball and allows room for it to come between him and the side.

3 He lets the ball come back a little further than for the drive and, slowing his swing, angles it into the side wall.

Reverse angle

1 For the reverse angle, the player will endeavour to adopt a position with the ball between himself and the front wall.

2 He leaves the ball sitting out more in front of him than for a cross-court and uses a full swing as this helps provide some disguise.

3 The player brings his swing down close to his body and, if necessary, will improvise with the wrist.

Stuart Hailstone of Scotland plays a defensive backhand boast to draw Chris Robertson of Australia forward off the 'T'

4 This shot is a fine variation to use and, if not overplayed, can surprise an opponent who is anticipating a drive.

4 The target is an angle into the side wall that will keep the ball as close to the front as possible on the rebound.

reach the front wall. However, it is possible to play angles delicately, fading them into the front wall, so to speak, but this requires special skill and there are not many players who do it well – not that you should be deterred from trying, of course. Like all shots requiring touch, they must be played with slower racket speed, but still purposefully. Delicately does not mean weakly.

When to play angles is a tactically significant consideration. It is true to say that when players are making imprudent shot selections, the angle figures regularly. There may not be much choice about when you play the defensive angle and it is probably better to straighten the ball up whenever possible. The reverse angle and the short angle are shots that will provide you with several options; therefore, they should always be played with your opponent's position in mind. The relatively small number of players with a particular ability to play angles will, because of that ability, tend to select the occasion to play them more wisely.

An angle does, of course, have the advantage of turning an opponent and, like a drop shot, bringing an opponent into the front of the court, which will increase physical pressure. So whereas a fresh opponent may pick them up, one who is beginning to tire may have more difficulty; they will also make him even more tired. An appropriate time, therefore, to introduce angles is when you feel your opponent is weakening physically. This requires a perceptive quality some players do not have, as they play cocooned in their problems; the ability to introduce angles almost at will is by no means easy.

The repertoire of those who play angles well is greatly enhanced and they are invariably attractive to watch. Many of them are of a bygone age; they learned to play in the colder conditions that encouraged use of this type of shot. As the game has developed and playing conditions have become warmer, those learning the game are naturally less disposed to experiment with angles. However, whatever the conditions, they cannot be ignored and need to be part of your regular practice sessions. In this way, at least when you have to play them, they are at your disposal.

The drop shot

The drop shot is an essential attacking shot, principally designed to work your opponent into the physically damaging and vulnerable front corners of the court. It can also be used to win a rally when you have put your opponent in a disadvantageous position.

The first shot may be described as a working drop; it should be as low as possible over the tin and will normally run, though not far, close to the side wall, forcing the opponent to play the ball close to the wall. The working drop shot will not be aimed at the nick with a view to ending the rally, since it will not be played from a position allowing this to happen. Obviously if the shot is played loosely, it will be of little value and will leave the opponent with ample opportunity to attack.

The drop designed to end the rally will be directed towards the nick with the aim of getting the ball to roll along the floor. Even if it fails to do this, it will be very difficult to retrieve if played well enough. Drops directed at the nick will be more successfully played if they are struck from wider positions and thus angled towards the nick.

The two drop shots already described will be played mostly from forward positions in the court, from where the opportunity to attack is best presented. However, both shots, more particularly the working drop shot, can be played from deeper in the court, though it goes without saying that this involves more risk. Some players become, with practice, more adept from deeper positions, especially on the backhand side.

The touch required for such shots comes by no means easily to many players. To those who find the touch difficult to acquire, practice is crucial; those with natural touch will still need to exercise their skills.

For most players, the forehand side, as with most other shots, provides more difficulty for the drop shot and there are very few players who are skilled at playing the drop shot from deep in the court on that side. Again the problems are related to

Forehand drop

1 Here the player shapes to the side of the ball for a straight drop. For this particular shot, his high backswing allows him to cut down on the ball.

2 Moving the racket through towards impact the player will slow his swing to provide some touch, allowing the ball to 'drop' off the front wall and bounce to cling.

3 Here the player uses a firm wrist and compact follow-through. Note how the racket is held open, showing that he has imparted considerable cut to the shot.

poor positioning. It is much more complicated to get into suitably balanced positions to play drop shots on the forehand side and it is from unbalanced positions that errors occur.

Potential problems with the racket are the dropping of the wrist and therefore the racket head on the backhand side, as well as overcutting a shot that already has a degree of natural cut. On the forehand side, low carriage and late preparation of the racket head will cause difficulties and, whichever side you are playing down, deviations of the wrist will clearly have dire consequences.

Drop shots, as we have seen, can be played from anywhere in the court provided competence allows; and, although straight drops will be played far more frequently, the cross-court drop has its own value. It is played almost exclusively to win the point outright, either for the cross-court nick or for the space created when an opponent is aligned directly behind you.

Awareness of when to play the shot is of particular significance, since if the wrong selection is made, the shot may be played into the path of the opponent or an attempt for the cross-court nick may be made off a ball that is unsuitable. It is sensible, therefore, to experiment with drop shots in practice or during practice games, rather than attempting them in matches before they have become secure in your repertoire.

The satisfaction to be gained from making shots with a high degree of difficulty is considerable and, once experienced, should serve as an encouragement to persist with them.

Susan Devoy of New Zealand, one of the game's greatest exponents of the backhand drop shot, can lure opponents forward, drive them backwards, cross-court or kill straight to the nick from almost identical preparation practically anywhere on the court

The drop shot

This, in turn, will greatly increase your own confidence in your ability to execute the shots successfully.

Drops so far discussed have been played off balls that have bounced, but there is no reason why drop shots should not be played off the volley. For most players, this is a more difficult proposition, but some will have a penchant for them and practice always helps. Being able to cut off volleys in mid-court and drop them in short will provide alternatives to hitting the ball more firmly and into the back of the court. If you are able to show your opponent that you have options, he will feel less secure and for good reason.

So the drop shot, whether straight or cross-court, whether off the bounce or off the volley, provides contrast in pace and placement to the hard-hit ball. Mastery, or at least reasonable control, of the drop shot is therefore essential to a well-rounded game. Without it, limitations are exposed and it will not require an opponent of exceptional awareness to recognize that the drop shot is not part of your armoury. He will soon realize that he can lie back in the court, moving in the less strenuous lateral directions rather than front to back, which sooner or later takes its toll even on the fittest players. He also knows that he can put you into the front areas of the court, without feeling too vulnerable.

Players often excuse themselves from playing the drop by admitting that it is a shot they cannot play. That is understandable, but very negative. If you cannot play a drop shot, practise it and then employ it in game situations of a less crucial nature until you feel more confident. Reluctance to attempt the shot will lead you nowhere.

The ability to play the drop shot, apart from making you a more effective player, will make you eminently more watchable. There are few shots that are more appealing to the spectator than a well-executed drop shot; and apart from improving your spectator appeal it will do your opponent untold physical damage, which will enhance your prospects of winning.

Backhand drop

1 Here the player positions himself slightly forward and uses a high backswing that enables him to impart cut to the ball.

2 The racket has come down to cut across the back of the ball.

3 The target area for the cross-court drop is the nick. Cross-court drops can be played firmly with a compact and rhythmic swing across the body.

The lob

The lob, like the drop, falls into the category of touch shots, since it requires similar delicate control of the racket. It is a shot that often seems to be underused, particularly in view of the fact that it serves so many different purposes.

Essentially, it is played as a defensive shot and is designed to give you time to recover from troublesome situations. But, in the same way as the deep angle, if you judge it precisely, the lob can end up being an outright winner, particularly in cooler conditions where the ball may stop in the back of the court. Moreover, if an opponent puts you under pressure into the front corners the lob may be your most effective means of working your way back into the rally. It is also a shot that lends itself to being played when you are at full stretch.

The lob is mostly played cross-court and must be played with both height and width. If it is not high enough it will be a simple matter for your centrally-placed opponent to capitalize on the situation; lack of width may cause similar problems as, once again, the lob will be easy to intercept. An inferior lob is therefore very vulnerable and may lose you the rally, just as a superior one may put you back in the game.

The width required is similar to the width required off the service. The ball should make contact with the side wall deep in the court, so that it forces your opponent into playing an angle, or even better, making it unplayable.

If the cross-court lob is underplayed, the straight lob or 'floater' is played even less often. It is a very worthwhile shot, since not only does it have the advantages of the cross-court equivalent, but played well it will be close to the side wall, creating all sorts of problems for your opponent. It is most interesting that the latest sensation in world squash, Jansher Khan, uses the shot frequently and tellingly. He also lobs cross-court, but in his classic semi-final with Jahangir Khan in the World Championships at the NEC in Birmingham, England, it was his use of the straight lob that most caught the eye. He was very adept at hoisting the ball straight, pacelessly, when the ball had passed his body. He played the shot in an improvised manner that would be difficult to imitate and which is probably beyond the average player.

Jansher Khan plays the front forehand corner with great variation. At full stretch, he can produce a straight drop or lob, or lob cross-court

Although idiosyncratic, the shot lacked nothing in accuracy, since almost without exception it had the virtues of closeness to the wall and height.

The lob is one of those essential shots that assist players in varying pace. The majority of shots in squash are hit quite firmly, so the more delicate ones such as the drop and lob, apart from breaking up the shape of any rally, add the important ingredient of change of pace. Variety of shot is more obvious and may be more attractive to the spectator than change

The lob

of pace, which is a far more subtle tactic. But do not underrate its value. It has the distinct advantage of preventing opponents from establishing a rhythm.

Many players, especially those who like to hit the ball consistently, are thrown out of joint by more delicate shots such as the lob. It is no easy matter to force the pace off shots that themselves have no pace in them. A parallel can be drawn with the game of cricket: the batsman can use the pace of a quick bowler to assist his striking power, but he will have to use more force to generate the same power off a slow bowler. The hitters in squash will therefore be tempted by lobs, will quicken the rhythm of their swings, snatching at the ball and making errors.

As already mentioned, the lob may often be played under pressure, at full stretch. Difficult though this may sound, provided good balance is maintained, it may even assist the technical requirements of the shot such as opening up the racket face to lift the ball high on to the front wall. Failure to do this, and many players do have problems with it, will clearly mean that the lob has insufficient height. If the racket face is opened up too much it may mean that the ball goes high out of the court. This error will be made more likely if the racket movement through the ball is too sudden and jerky. Circumstances allowing, it is best if the lob is played with a full controlled swing, keeping the wrist firm. However, it is a shot that may be improvised with a flick of the wrist when pressure decrees.

To play the lob well it is necessary, at the front of the court, to bend down low. This will help you get under the ball, which is difficult from upright positions. Although the shot will be played mostly from the front of the court, it can in fact be played from anywhere. Indeed, Jansher Khan, as previously stated, plays the straight lob from positions deep in the court when the ball has passed him. Some players, for example Lisa Opie, are adept at lobbing off the opponent's serve when it is met on the volley.

Forehand lob

1 Lunging for the ball, the racket is prepared in a low backswing with an open racket face, allowing the swing to get under the ball and lift it high on to the front wall.

2 At impact the racket is very open and moving upwards. Note that the player has come in behind the ball for this cross-court shot.

3 The follow-through shows clearly the upward path of the swing which will have given the ball height on the front wall.

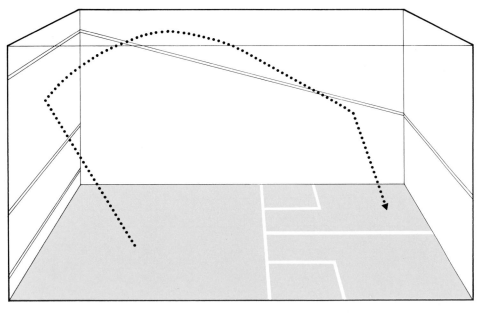

The lob must be played with both width and height. The ball's ideal trajectory should take it to the side wall deep in the court

Lisa plays this shot particularly well on the backhand, which is by no means an easy matter.

If the lob does not come naturally, then practise it, for you will find it a valuable weapon that enables you to gain recovery time and to change the pace of your game.

Forehand or backhand, lob returns of serve seem bread-and-butter matters to Lisa Opie. Others might need determined practice

Backhand lob

1 The player positions himself to the side of the ball for a straight lob.

2 Under a little pressure, he has to get down under the ball to attain height. Again, note the open racket face.

3 Even under pressure, good balance has been maintained and the player has good racket control on the follow-through.

The service

One of the main problems in squash is that you have an opponent who hits every other ball. Unlike many sports you are directly affected by your opponent's every move. The ice skater seeks perfection; the skier looks to beat the clock; the swimmer is only indirectly affected by his opposition; but the squash player will often only be able to do what his opponent allows. We all know that rather helpless feeling of being outplayed: the opponent manipulates us like a puppet and we seem to be permanently on the defensive, unable to assert ourselves long enough to assume positions of attack.

It is therefore important to take full advantage of those situations in which you are able to exert some form of control. The serve is just such an instance; it is in your own hands and up to you to make the best job of it you can. Your opponent may, by the positions he takes up, threaten your serve; he may, by what he achieves with his return of service, make you feel less comfortable about the prospect of serving, but it is still up to you. It is therefore in your interests to develop a serve that gives you as much of an advantage as possible, and one that at least puts you at no disadvantage.

When a player is in the beginners' class, it is likely that he will concentrate on the serve. There are two good reasons: firstly, he will need to be able to serve to begin a rally; and secondly, the better the serve is, as a beginner, the more problems it will cause for opponents who are also beginners. They will be at some disadvantage with a serve that reaches them high on the volley and at an even greater disadvantage should the ball end up in the corners. It is not, however, in the beginner's interest to get obsessed by the serve; it is far more important to develop an ability to play rallies. Once you reach a certain playing standard, the serve appears to become less significant. However, this is not the case; at the more advanced levels of the game, you have to become more

Service from right-hand box

1 The player positions herself for the serve by pointing her toes into and facing the front corner, allowing her to stroke smoothly across the body and into the centre of the front wall.

2 The player uses a low backswing and an open racket face to come under the ball.

3 She lets her weight move through comfortably with the shot and lifts the ball up high on to the front wall with a firm and compact swing.

With his serve, Jahangir Khan will endeavour to put the ball tight on to the side wall, beating Umar Hayat's volley and forcing him into a difficult retrieval in the back corner

aware of the serve, since opponents of an equally high standard will deal ruthlessly with a weak serve.

The service in squash will never be as important as it is in tennis, nor will it ever be as technically difficult. The first priority is to establish a basic serve that you are able to produce consistently. Once that is established, you can look to develop one or two variations.

The basic serve should be of sufficient height and width to reach the side wall far enough back in the court, so that if it bounces, it lands in the back corners. That would be ideal, but it is at least as important to make sure that you do not present your

Service from left-hand box

1 From the left box, the player faces the opposite side wall and steps along the short line. Again, she will use a low backswing with an open racket face.

2 For the lob or semi-lob serve, the player will come under and up through the ball.

3 Here, she strokes smoothly across the body and lifts the ball high on to the front wall. A firm wrist will aid control.

The service

opponent with a serve that reaches him conveniently on the volley. Few serves will be easier to deal with. Nor should the serve hit the side wall too early, leaving it 'short' in the court. That will present your opponent with an easy shot and plenty of room in which to play.

Equally, it is undesirable for the serve to hit the side wall too firmly. That will have the effect of bringing the ball out towards the middle of the court. The receiver will then have every right to move out to make room for his return of serve, at the same time preventing you, quite legitimately, from moving to the centre of the court. It hardly needs to be said that serving out is not excusable.

Service and movement to 'T'

Variations on a basic serve can be achieved by changes of pace, however slight, and there is always value in a harder-hit serve in the style of the Rackets serve. The harder-hit serve aimed directly at the receiver is effective and often used in the top-class game. Not many players are adept at playing the ball off the body or even close to the body.

Some players, though there are not many left, are expert at the lob serve, but unless you belong to this category it is unwise to flirt with the lines. What will help you to deliver a worthwhile serve is proper preparation. Take your time in the service box, do not rush, and focus on what you are attempting to do. An accurate serve

may well determine the shape of the rally, putting you immediately into an advantageous position and your opponent under pressure. Jonah Barrington is a fine exponent of the serve and Jansher Khan also has a fine serve. If it is important enough for *them* to take trouble with it, it is certainly important enough for you.

There are certain advantages to be gained whichever side you elect to serve from. If you serve from the right-hand box, the position you adopt assists in making a suitable angle on to the left-hand side wall. However, you are serving with your back to your opponent and you must be aware of the need to turn and watch. When serving from the left-hand box

1 The player positions herself and prepares for the service, pausing momentarily to gain composure before serving.

2 She prepares her racket and uses a low underarm throw to create time for a smooth swing.

3 The racket is brought under and up through the ball.

In preparing to serve, Ross Thorne of Australia demonstrates excellent racket preparation and total concentration on the ball

you will have your opponent in full view; this is of considerable benefit, but it is probably more difficult to achieve a more testing angle on to the side wall.

Also to be taken into account is your opponent's ability to deal with the serve more efficiently on a particular side. Most players automatically serve to their opponent's backhand without considering whether or not they are strong on that side, and many are.

In short, do not merely accept the serve as a means of putting the ball into play. You must be aware of the advantages you may gain from accurate serving as well as the harm you may do yourself if you serve badly.

4 As she completes the service, the player starts her movement towards the 'T'.

5 She does not stop after the serve but continues her movement to the ready position.

6 From the ready position, the player will watch her opponent and her service, and be ready to anticipate her opponent's return.

Return of service

As the receiver your first contribution to any rally will be the return of serve and, since you are likely to be receiving at least as often as you are serving, it is equally as important as the serve. How well you are able to return will depend almost as much on your own ability as on the quality of the serve.

The server will be trying to contain your return of service so that you are unable to make a winning shot and, if possible, to put you into the disadvantageous areas. The first requirement is to get the ball into play and one of the main difficulties, if the service is testing, is judging the precise moment when to play the ball. It should be your aim, where possible, to get on to the volley or play the ball after it has bounced, but before it reaches the difficult deep areas. If you are able to play the ball freely after the serve has bounced, this indicates that the serve is not a particularly demanding one.

If the serve is accurate and reaches the side wall where it is a problem, deep in the court and on the side wall, you have to decide when to attempt to play the ball. If you can make the volley before it reaches the side wall, without feeling too pressed or un-

Forehand volley return

1 In the position for receiving service, the player stands a racket length behind the corner of the service box, facing the front corner of the court and watching the server.

2 She will prepare her racket and move into position as soon as she has decided on her best option for returning service.

3 The player prepares for a straight forehand volley return with good racket preparation and by positioning to the side of the ball.

comfortable, this is a sensible course of action. Once the ball has made contact with the side wall, the next option is to volley after the contact. This

Jahangir Khan winds up a powerful drive volley return of service, aiming to drag his opponent into the deep backhand court

necessitates a revision of position: you must move away from the side wall to allow room for the racket. Failure to do so – and this is a common failing – will lead to mistiming or at worst missing the ball altogether. For the beginner this shot causes problems, as does the whole area of when to attempt to play the serve. Awareness of the possibilities and experience of dealing with them will bring

4 Having prepared well, she waits for the ball to fall to the best point before striking.

5 As the racket is coming under and up through the ball it shows that the return is aimed high on the front wall to achieve good length.

6 A straight good-length return, whether on the volley or a drive, is the standard return of serve. It will enable the receiver to move to the dominant position on the 'T'.

Return of service

about improvement.

Failure to volley either before or after the ball has hit the side wall leaves you with the final option, the angle. Although your opponent will be happy enough to see you forced into playing a defensive angle, all is not lost if you play it well. Once the necessary judgment is acquired and a level of competence in returning the serve achieved, then other possibilities and variations will become available.

Once you have acquired the technical ability to return the service, you can turn your attention to where best to place the ball. Basically, the options are straight or cross-court, low or high, deep or short, with angles added for variation. Logically, the most effective returns are straight, since they are furthest from the server, but like all straight shots they will need to be close to the wall, and running along the wall. The more they stray, the more vulnerable they become. Effective serving may make straight returns more difficult and may force you into going cross-court. Width and depth, therefore, are crucial, for a weak cross-court return will be very easy to attack.

Playing in short off the service will bring its own rewards, if it succeeds

High backhand volley return

1 The player is in the receiving position for what will probably be a backhand return.

2 Preparation for what is anticipated to be a high backhand volley return of service.

3 She positions herself to the side, turning the shoulder, to prepare for a straight return.

in forcing your opponent into the front of the court; but it is no simple matter to play such shots and, if you try and fail with a couple, be chary of persisting. A series of errors off the service will do wonders for your opponent's morale. Sensible selection and discretion, once technique is established, are of paramount importance. These will be acquired through the awareness that experience brings.

4 The player shows excellent preparation, waiting for the ball to fall to the anticipated impact point.

5 The racket has moved down and is about to move up through the ball to lift it high on to the front wall for a straight return to good length.

6 By volleying the return of serve, the receiver avoids the problem of having to get the ball out of the back corners. She then moves to the 'T'.

Match report **FLAIR AND SKILL**

Event: Blue Stratos British Under-23 Open Final
Venue: The Oasis, Marlow, Buckinghamshire, UK
Date: 24 January, 1986
Scoreline: Rodney Martin (Australia) bt Zarak Jahan (Pakistan)
5–9 6–9 9–0 9–3 9–6

For years the name of the game in squash was percentage play. Barrington, Hunt, Jahangir Khan and Ross Norman, all talented shot-makers in their own right, stifled their wilder inclinations in favour of victory through attrition. With phenomenal training and relentless retrieving, they developed the successful tactic of wearing down their opponents over two hours or more before applying the coup de grâce.

A generation grew up behind these great players, bored by the prospect of a complete career in such confinement and equipped with both the technique and the tools to take another, more adventurous route. Oddly enough, the best of these arose in the Australian Institute of Squash in Brisbane, under the stern direction of Geoff Hunt.

The man who sounded the death knell upon the philosophy of attritional play was Rodney Martin, and he did it in the final of the Blue Stratos British Under-23 Open Championships, at Marlow in Buckinghamshire on 24 January, 1986.

The outside world first heard murmurs about Rodney Martin when he won a particularly weak Australian Open Championship earlier in the same season, beating Hunt who was then nearing his fourth decade. It was a freak result, according to the grapevine, and anyway there was an elder brother, Brett, who was the real talent of the Martin family.

In fact there was a whole family of squash-playing Martins, based at their commercial club in Engadine, near Sydney, New South Wales. The elder Martins were both NSW state players. Brett was a renowned on-court adventurer capable of removing anyone from a tournament when his cavalier dedication to shot-making was grooving well. At the Institute in Brisbane a beautiful younger sister, Michelle, was preparing for her own entrance upon the world circuit.

Rodney Martin was seeded fifth at Marlow on the strength of his Australian win, but he was not regarded very seriously in a field that included Fredrik Johnson of Sweden, Sohail Qaiser of Pakistan, Jamie Hickox of England and a clutch of experienced young national league regulars from all over Britain.

The fourth seed was equally unknown to British observers of the game. Zarak Jahan is the younger Pakistani brother of England's Hiddy Jahan. He had been quietly slipping across from Quetta to Hiddy's home in Croydon for several summers of coaching and had established a little-known professional base at the Blarney Club in Ireland. His seeding appeared to be based on a recent win in the Open Des Canaux in France and great respect for his antecedents.

Before the week was out at Marlow, these two had put down firm roots for future international careers and set a playing trend that revolutionized the game on a worldwide scale.

Zarak Jahan was the new face of attritional play. A small-framed eighteen-year-old with a surprisingly strong arm, his game was based upon astonishing powers of retrieval. At Marlow he seemed the fastest thing seen around a court since Jahangir Khan was a youngster, with a splits-stretch to all four corners of the court that was painful just to watch. He went through the field like a knife, beating Ahmed Tahir of Egypt, Grant Way of South Africa, Johnathan Clark of Durham, Paul Symonds of South Africa and Johnson, the Swede who had beaten his brother in an early round of the previous British Open.

Martin arrived at the head of a strong Australian Institute contingent and was almost ignored by observers in favour of flashier performers such as Austin Adarraga and Philip Larmer. He pegged his way to the final, beating Ireland's Jeffrey Hearst, John Clark of Wiltshire, Paul Carter of Hertfordshire, Sohail Qaiser and Robert Owen of Warwickshire.

At the start of the final there was little disagreement that the Marlow audience was about to see the launch of another Pakistani teenage machine to dominate the world behind Jahangir Khan. Zarak, with Hiddy in attendance and proudly discussing his obvious potential, looked too fast, too tough and generally too well prepared for the long-legged and rather self-effacing lad from Engadine.

The first two games of the final reinforced that view. Zarak set such a pace of fearless retrieval and counter-attack that the match began to look like a comprehensive whitewash. In just over half an hour Zarak was 9–5 9–6 in the lead and stepping jauntily on court with a smile to his brother that promised easy victory.

Three minutes later he was staggering out of the court door again, having lost the third game 9–0 in a single hand, and another ten minutes saw him fighting for survival at 2–2.

Martin hit ten nick shots in succes

Zarak Jahan in front and winning easily, until Rodney Martin hit ten successive nick shots in just three minutes to grab the initiative and steal the title

sion to take service from the confident little Pakistani and then finish the game almost without opposition. He won eleven points without interruption and then another eleven for only four points relinquished to establish a 4–0 lead in the fifth game. He did this by the simple yet devastatingly adventurous ploy of abandoning the patient rallying with which Zarak had shown he could live for the rest of the night, and going for outright kill shots at every opportunity.

It was a moment of self-revelation for the Brisbane-based Sydneysider. In his early days total familiarity with the game and its environment on his home courts bred exactly this kind of arrogant dependence upon flair and skill with the new generation of light-weight but extremely powerful graphite rackets.

'A year with Geoff Hunt taught me to harness my natural racket skills,' Martin explained later. 'I used to just go out on court and fire at everything. It was good enough to a certain level, but a good retriever with a class game in his own racket arm could always knock me out of a long match, and often could win quickly if my shots were slightly off. Geoff put discipline in my game, made me rally patiently from a base of physical fitness, looking for the gaps into which I could fire my shots to best advantage.

'But two games down to Zarak I had no options left. I was sure as hell going to lose trying to match his rallying power, so I reached for the shots the way I used to.'

Martin won 9–6 in the fifth after sixty-six minutes of play. He won ten points in the third and fourth games,

cutting the ball straight to the top left nick from every part of the court. With an advanced, Pakistani-style grip on the racket, the speed to cover the court to arrive balanced for almost every shot, a forearm strong enough to convert his preparation to any covering move from his opponent, Martin is impossible to read accurately in the front of the court and totally unpredictable in the deep corners.

Within months he was a force to be reckoned with on the world circuit and other youngsters, attracted by the flair and daring of his style, perhaps also by the laconic Australian humour with which he welcomed victory, began to practise the same style and technique. Attrition was

never again to be quite so highly valued.

Rodney Martin went back to Marlow the following year and treated an older, stronger and even more determined Zarak Jahan to the same lesson. If that might seem merely to suggest domination of one player and one style of play, he took on the mighty Jahangir Khan himself in the final of the New South Wales Open in July 1987, went two games down and then became only the second man in six years to beat the greatest player ever. He did it by reaching for the shots the way he used to, the way he had discovered was a legitimate option at a moment of crucial balance against superb opposition.

Chapter 3 PREPARATION AND PRACTICE

Thoughtful match preparation and constant practice are ways to boost confidence and enhance performance. It helps enormously if you can structure your practice and formulate a personalized training plan. Preparation can be either short or long term. Long-term preparation should aim continually to increase physical fitness and improve racket skills. It should heighten your ability to identify your strengths and weaknesses and remedy faults, and to perfect racket and ball co-ordination. Valuable practice includes learning to move effectively around the court, position yourself well and anticipate your opponent's next move. Short-term preparation concentrates on the match to be played. It is important to warm up and make the most of the knock-up; to prepare yourself mentally for the challenge ahead; to practise as many shots as possible and to look closely at your opponent's game for weaknesses. Diligent preparation reaps rewards; it can give you faith in your game and help you play more fluently.

Pre-match preparation

What you are able to do in preparing for matches will depend to a large extent on the time available to you. Professionals have fewer problems in this respect, but it is a different matter for those who work a normal day. If you are well prepared and know it, you will benefit from the confidence that thorough preparation brings.

Long-term preparation will give you a platform on which to base your season, so much of it will be done pre-season, that is in the summer in the UK. The warmer weather will make physical work more agreeable and, since courts play quicker in these conditions, there will be benefits from having to play sustained rallies. Winning rallies too quickly and too easily in cold playing conditions can give you a false sense of how easy the game is.

To obtain maximum advantage from long-term preparation it is important to know what your strengths and weaknesses are so that they can be brought into better harmony. The

Susan Devoy wins many of her vital matches on superior strength. It takes work to make strength

less athletic racket players may need to spend more time on the physical aspects of training; conversely, the athlete may need to improve his racket skills. It is a common failing to spend time on the things you do well, rather than remedying weaknesses, and it is no easy matter to know where your own problems lie. It is advisable,

therefore, if practical, to seek advice from an expert. In that way a balanced programme can be established.

The summer, less hindered or completely unhindered by matchplay, is the ideal time to work with longer-term objectives, since stamina training, for example, would impair your ability to play matches satisfactorily. Any heavier physical work is best done well in advance of the start of the season, so that it has time to take effect. This will also leave time for you to move into quicker, more sharpening work in the weeks immediately before the season begins. Physical work may take the form of running, exercises and weights, but, again, advice should be sought about the suitability of the work undertaken, so that it is fruitful and the possibility of injury is reduced. Short-term preparation may involve the days prior to any particular match and the day of the match itself.

Players will need to have an understanding of their own requirements to get the best out of themselves, if they are working without guidance. Some players thrive on a heavy workload, usually physical players or those who have been brought up to work hard;

Even the great Jahangir books court time with his coach and mentor, Rahmat Khan, to prepare and practise on the day of a vital match

others, often the lighter-weight players, will need less work and be more concerned about keeping themselves fresh.

Your preparation for any one particular match will depend on what has gone before: whether you feel you are playing well and whether you are winning your matches. If things are not going well, you will have to decide whether to redouble your efforts or whether a lighter schedule is necessary. Some players will gain confidence from hard work, but this may be counter-productive if it creates staleness. Equally, it is not wise to delude yourself into resting when in fact you are not putting in enough work.

On balance, hard work is perhaps the best alternative, but it has to be recognized that players are different in their needs. It is the understanding of your own needs and capabilities that is particularly difficult and this is an area where a good coach can help. Although only a few top squash professionals have personal coaches with them all the time – and this is largely a financially induced situation – it is clear how influential coaches are by looking at the top tennis players.

The day of any match will be important, though for someone working a normal day, matters will not always be under his control. When they are, he should control them. Although squash is often played as a provider of relief from the hurly-burly of a busy life, a heavy day at the office will not be conducive to a match-winning performance.

Since you will not always be able to determine whether or not you are going to have a difficult day, it will be worth cultivating the habit of switching off from the day's work on your way to the match. The worst thing you can do is to arrive hot and bothered and rush straight on court. This is a recipe for disaster and will almost certainly see you one or even two games down. It is best, therefore, to try to arrive for the match with time to settle yourself.

It is advisable, whenever it proves possible, to have a loosening hit, quite probably on your own on the day of the match. Lunch time, or more immediately before the match, may provide a suitable opportunity. A practice hit just before the match should prevent you from starting slowly and, since some players are habitual slow starters, they will need to warm up. If you are in this category, but have warmed up well and suddenly find yourself in the unusual situation of leading 2–0, that may prove difficult to cope with!

Apart from physical and playing preparation, you need to be as mentally prepared as possible. Be relaxed without being too relaxed; do not underrate opponents when you play at a lower level, if that is the situation, because it is often difficult to raise your game. To underrate opposition is an undesirable form of conceit.

Whatever else you may have done during the day of the match, the knock-up will still be important. It will be of even more importance if you have not hit a ball that day or have had only a limited opportunity to warm up physically. The five-minute knock-up will not be long in such undesirable circumstances, but it is better than nothing.

You will be unable to practise the whole range of your shots, always presuming you have a range, so the best thing you can do is to get the swing working, get the feet into position and generally liven up. Apart from the good you can do for yourself, the knock-up also gives you the chance to take stock of your opponent. You may be able to spot some of his more obvious weaknesses; but be aware that appearances in knock-ups can be deceptive. Sometimes the clumsiest, most inept-looking players in the knock-up turn out to be anything but. It is equally true that the stylists, at times, turn out to be ineffective once the action is for real.

If you happen to be one of those lucky players who can just turn up and play to form you are very fortunate indeed. For most, the pre-match build-up and preparation will be of far greater significance; be aware of this and do the best you can.

Defence and attack

Having established a technique that will allow you to play shots in a variety of circumstances, your attention needs to be directed towards the more tactical aspects of the game. Tactics, simply put, mean where you hit the ball as opposed to how. It would, of course, be of little use having unusual powers of awareness if your technique does not allow you to take advantage of them.

Some fortunate players have a natural awareness of space and where opponents are; others, less blessed, may have to learn and develop that important sense, since there is little value in hitting the ball back to your opponents. Tactics also involve the

appreciation of when to attack and when to defend and, though that may often appear obvious, there will certainly be times when defensive options are taken instead of attacking ones. The reverse will also be true, but much less often.

One of the worst aspects of modern sport is when players are afraid to attack; fear of losing, often imposed by misguided coaches, is a prime cause. However, defeat is usually still the outcome, and generally you will feel better if you have gone down attacking rather than having played negatively. English rugby union sides are an outstanding example of this point: for three-quarters of the match

they will not attempt to run the ball, even when their wings are their main strength, and will kick away hard-earned possession. Then, finding themselves behind in the last quarter, they will run the ball from almost anywhere and finish the match, making everyone ask why they had not liberated themselves earlier.

It is up to enlightened coaches to free their charges from this trait. That wonderful Irish centre, Mike Gibson, said that one of the best pieces of advice he had ever received was given by the late, revered Carwyn James, who told him never to be frightened of making a mistake. That advice, of course, is much easier to

Straight backhand from back corner

 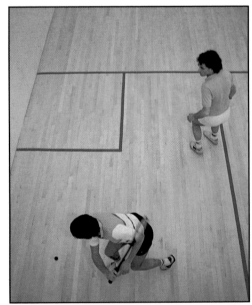

1 The player on the right has played a good-length drive which is allowing him to take up a dominant position on the 'T'.

2 The striker is forced into a defensive position in the back corners.

3 From the back corners the striker must play a defensive shot, aimed at forcing his opponent off the 'T' and into the back corners. He will achieve this with a straight length.

Ross Norman, about to exploit a rare opening against Jansher Khan by driving into created space in the forehand court

give to players with Gibson's talent, but it is worth giving to all sportsmen and women.

Once the attacking shot has been well practised and is part of your repertoire, all that needs to be sought is the right moment to play it. Far easier said than done, for selection of shot and opportunity does not come easily to everyone. When the right moment presents itself, it is best that nothing stops you taking advantage of it. The state of the particular game or match should not really come into it, though it would be true to say that it often influences matters.

There is a school of thought that advocates an attacking disposition when you are serving and a defensive one when you are out of hand. It makes good sense, but you may find it difficult to put into practice. Players rarely have the ability to alter the pattern of their games to any great extent, and to ask them to do so from rally to rally seems too much. Far better is to play each rally on its own merit, attempting to win each one, and seeing it only in relation to itself.

Attack is a desirable philosophy, but it is true to say that most successful teams or individuals have a firm foundation in their defensive abilities. The need for solid defence – you certainly will not win unless you can keep the ball in play – should not become obsessive, as it may lead to negative attitudes. This may be especially prevalent in squash players who are naturally athletic, and who consequently strive always to chase the ball up. To some extent the game lends itself to such a disposition; however, at times it can be a weakness in the game itself, rather like the need to be 7 feet tall to play basketball or 16 stone to play lock forward. Athleticism, however, is preferable to freakishness.

Part of playing any game, no matter what your standard, is the pleasure you derive from it; and you are more likely to get pleasure from attacking than defending. You are far more likely to wake up in the middle of the night remembering your drop shot into the nick than a simple straight ball down the side wall.

Problem areas of the court

It does no harm to sit back occasionally and consider the problem areas of the court. Played successfully, squash is about putting the ball, and thus your opponent, into these difficult areas.

Logically, the four corners make obvious appeal: if you put the ball into the front corners, you have brought your opponent into forward positions from which he has, unless he can win the rally outright, little chance to recover. The accumulative effect of such movements will put your opponent under the sort of physical pressure that you will be able to take advantage of sooner or later. Remember, however, that, as in all these instances, he will be attempting to do the same to you.

Driving your opponent into the back corners may not have such serious physical consequences, but he may be hard-pressed to make worthwhile returns from such positions. If you contain your opponent in the back corners, you will soon find opportunities to attack.

No matter where your opponent finds himself in the court, he will have trouble playing a ball that runs close to the wall. So this will always be a priority. The further the ball is from the side wall, the more accessible it will be to your opponent, and the more it strays the more vulnerable it will be to interception.

A more specific area that causes acute difficulty is the point on the side wall where an ideal serve, or indeed an ideal lob, would make contact – deep in the court, behind the service box and as close to the cut line as you dare.

The nick, which is the point where the wall and the floor join, is a problem area, though not one you can do much about if your opponent puts the

Straight forehand from back corner

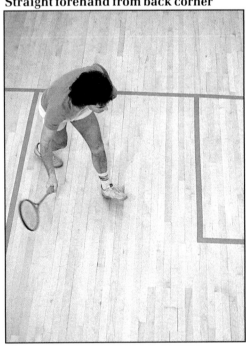

1 It is important when striving to retrieve the ball from the back corners to turn and face the back corner. Note how the player is already starting to prepare his racket.

Playing the ball into the problem areas of the court will put pressure on your opponent and force him into a difficult retrieval. But remember, he will be attempting to do the same to you

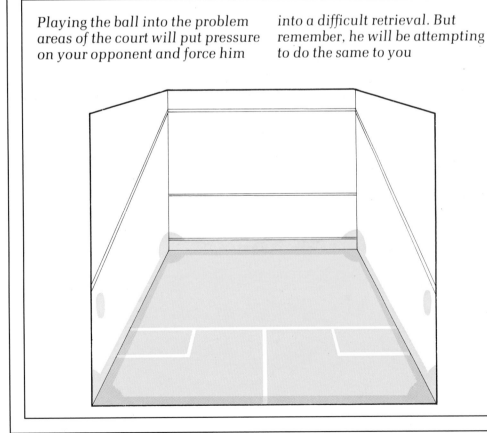

Jahangir Khan moves smoothly to the 'T' while Phil Kenyon contrives a cramped retrieval of the drive to the deep backhand corner

ball in it. Exactly played, the shot will be unreturnable. It will soon become clear if your opponent has the ability to play such shots. It will then be up to you to limit his opportunities.

Nicks are the most deadly and final of all shots, designed to bring rallies to an end. To have the ability to find the nick is invaluable, since to be a 'finisher' is an advantage of incalculable significance. To end rallies by hitting the ball away not only wins points, but it shortens rallies, thereby saving energy. It also disturbs your opponent's peace of mind and increases your own confidence.

2 The player does not move directly to the ball, but to a position to the side.

3 The player strives to get behind and to the side of the ball so that at the impact point the racket makes a right angle with the side wall. He will then be able to play a straight drive.

4 The swing must come down, under and up through the ball and lift it above the cut line to achieve a straight length return.

Common faults and weaknesses

It is useful to be aware of the weaknesses and faults that commonly recur in the course of any one game of squash. Being aware will enable you to work at remedying them on a long-term basis and avoiding them in matchplay.

Positioning and racket control are the two principal areas where faults may be easily identified. The need to take up good positions is always important and failure to do so will lead to inferior shots and errors. It may be that, under pressure, you are unable to address the ball in the most advantageous manner, but when the pressure is less intense every effort should be made to get into a balanced, comfortable position. This will enable shots you have at your disposal to be played. Common failings in positioning are: getting too close to the ball, leaning away from the ball and, worst of all, not being in a still, controlled position as you prepare to strike it.

Many sports involve chasing the ball and playing it close to the body and there is a danger of this spreading to squash. Nowhere is this more clearly illustrated than when players follow the ball into the back corners, ending up on top of the ball with no room to manoeuvre the racket. The answer is that, as you run back, you must keep away from the ball, thus allowing room for the swing. Pulling away from the ball is also caused by getting too close to it. It will lead to

moderate shots, often too high, or to errors. Pulling away from the ball is particularly prevalent on the forehand side deep in the court, especially on the angle. It has the added disadvantage of looking ungainly. Pulling away from the ball also occurs in

the front of the court off hard-hit balls. In no sport is it desirable to draw off the ball, thereby lifting the head and, at the same time, taking your eye off the ball.

Of all the aspects of positioning the most crucial is to be still and well-set

With the feet in correct alignment to the ball, the racket up and ready, and the body well set for the moment of strike, the chances of a correct stroke are greatly improved

Jahangir Khan bends the knees and waist to facilitate the perfect volley drop to the top backhand corner

at the moment of striking the ball. Moving as you play the ball is the worst of all technical deficiencies and will lead to more mistakes than any other single failing. Not being still includes running on through the ball and, apart from making it difficult to play a worthwhile shot, it creates the added difficulty of having to recover position, having to run further than you need and not being still enough to provide leverage for recovery.

Playing too upright is another common failing. Depending on the height .of the ball, bending, especially on the low shots is vitally important. Tall men in particular need to be aware of the importance of bending, otherwise they will certainly be caught out by shots such as low volleys.

When you take up a central position, you must be in a state of preparation in order to move to any part of the court. This need will not be best served if you assume too square a stance in the centre of the court, square to the front wall. An even distribution of weight on both feet does not help you to move. It is far better to have one foot in front of the other.

The game is best played wherever possible with a stance sideways to the front wall. Opening up the leading shoulder and ending up square to the front wall is undesirable. Invariably such a stance will cause you to make contact with the ball too early, bringing it back at yourself or out into the middle of the court.

It is important to know where to position yourself in set positions, such as receiving service. Many players stand too far back which lessens their chance of making a volley, as well as allowing the ball to get into the back corners. Equally some players stand too wide, that is, too far towards the centre of the court. This will also prevent them from volleying. It is rare for players to stand too close to the side walls when receiving service. Positioning yourself too close to the side wall is a weakness since it restricts the swing as well as alienating you from the middle of the court.

Rushing generally, and quickness of swing, can cause you to snatch at the ball and are therefore to be avoided at all costs. It is sound advice to take your time, especially when serving, as this will enable you to preserve the necessary composure.

Preparation of the racket head is a crucial matter and causes particular problems on the forehand, where it tends to be less thorough than on the backhand. The dangers of not having the racket up and ready are that you will be unprepared to play the ball and will swing on an incorrect line. The answer is to have the racket up and ready. In this way you will be better placed to play balls hit directly at you or ones that come at you sharply.

The wrist, or failure to control it, is another source of error. The dropping of the wrist will take the racket head down with it, causing an assortment of problems. Turning the wrist over leads to the closing of the racket face, which will inevitably result in the ball being struck into the tin; opening the wrist has the effect of opening the racket face which will cause high, uncontrolled shots that at worst go out of court. Watch any match of moderate, or even sometimes reasonable, standard and you will see all of these deviations of the wrist. The further up

Common faults and weaknesses

the playing scale, the less likely it is that you will see basic errors caused by an uncontrolled wrist; and, at the top levels, players hardly ever make mistakes of this kind, unless they are under extreme pressure.

Awareness of these common faults and weaknesses should help you to avoid them in matchplay, but your prospects will improve if you practise regularly to master the techniques. One of the pleasures to be derived from any sport, apart from the actual playing of the game, is improvement. There is often a great deal of dissatisfaction in feeling that you are not fulfilling your potential, and it is common to hear players say, 'If only I had started when I was younger.' It is much less common to hear them say, 'If only I had practised more.'

However, it is practice that will bring about improvement. It is unsatisfactory to know that your backhand is weak, that you cannot play a

drop shot, and to do nothing about it. It is most unlikely that you will produce a shot you are unsure of under the pressure of matchplay. If you are intent on improvement, merely to play games, whether they be friendlies or league matches, is not the answer. You are only liable to reproduce your technical shortcomings and errors repeatedly. Nor is it desirable to play with the same person time and again, however pleasurable the experience may be. People's games only vary minutely from match to match, and there is going to be little difference between games played with the same opponent.

To increase your chances of improvement, play a variety of opponents so that you learn to deal with a variety of situations. It is also more *challenging* to be confronted with different opponents. Finding a variety of opponents should not be a problem: internal leagues and the

social benefits of any well-run club should provide ample opportunity.

Since practice is so crucial to improvement it is important to find likeminded players who also realize its value. Older players, who tend to be more set in their ways, may not see practice as worthwhile; indeed, they may even be suspicious of it. However, once converted, some get hooked. Other players believe that practice cannot be worthwhile physically, but they can only be described as misguided.

It may well be that the best chance of a practice partner may come from the younger ranks. There is every chance that some of the younger players, if they are of a reasonable standard, will have had the benefit of coaching at club or county level or even at area or national level. Practising will be second nature to them.

Once you have someone to practise with, it will be useful to know as many routines as possible in order to cover all types of shot and to preserve freshness. The greater the variety of the practice and practice partners, the more enjoyable and profitable everything becomes. The routines that follow by no means represent a comprehensive list, but they cover all the essential shots and incorporate most of those you would be required to play during the course of a game. With a like-minded practice partner and carried out regularly, either as practice only or as a prelude to playing a game, these practices will without doubt bring rewards. It is well worth re-emphasizing that it is futile to practise without the required concentration and precision.

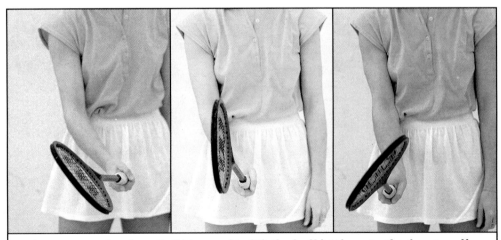

An open racket face (left) is used to lift the ball high on to the front wall, and also to apply cut. The flat racket face (centre) is used to hit the ball horizontally. The closed racket face (right) is used to hit down on the ball

Hitting straight combined with drop shot

To be able to hit the ball straight and accurately sounds relatively simple, but to achieve a sufficient degree of consistency is no easy matter. The more time spent perfecting the shot the better. Even when you appear to have the shot under control, it will still require regular practice.

In this practice, the straight hitter will work from a central position in the court, just ahead of the mid-court line. He will move into the front of the court to play his shot, recovering each time to his starting position. He should lead off his front foot.

The player who plays the drop shot will be in the back of the court, just behind the service box. He will attempt to play as good a drop shot as possible off his partner's straight hit. It is important to make the required adjustment to the feet and to play sideways to the front wall whenever possible. The straight hit should be relatively low, close to the wall and running down the wall into the corner without touching it. The drop shot should be light and low over the tin, and also close to the wall.

It is a waste of time to practise unless you concentrate and focus on accuracy and precision. It is only by practising in this way that the shots can be brought into matchplay. Players should, of course, perform both shots on both sides of the court.

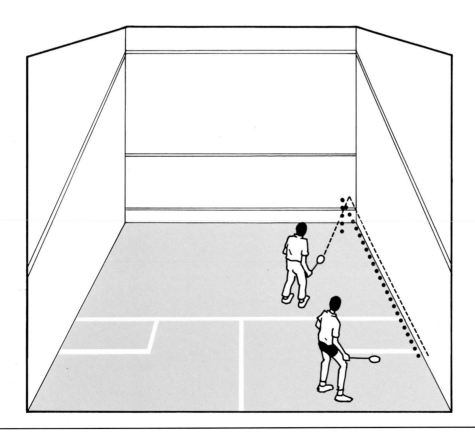

Common faults and weaknesses

Straight hit combined with angle with movement
This practice is widely used, but is rarely done properly, in which case it is worthless. It has the advantage of bringing in movement, though not of an excessive nature. One of the important aspects of this practice is to build up easy, rhythmical movement.

The front-court player hits the ball straight and low, running close to the wall; from a position behind the service box, the back-court player plays an angle, low and wide. Hitting high angles is a complete waste of time. Both players have sufficient time to concentrate both on easy movement and on correct positioning,

which should consist of front-foot leads.

If the shots are hit very accurately, it may mean that the rhythm of practice is disturbed. There is no need for concern, however, since the percentage of precise shots will not be high. Of the four shots involved in this practice, by far the worst is the forehand angle. Players invariably assume the wrong position, back-footed and leaning away from the ball. Now is the right time to improve technique in this area. This practice is also useful as a warm-up, or as preparation for a longer session of practice, but this is no reason for slackness.

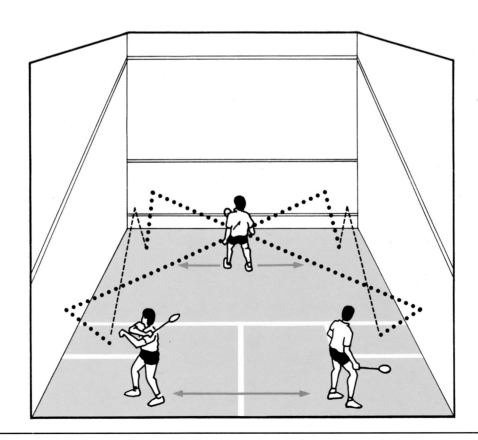

Cross-court hit and angle

Hitting straight, as we have seen, is an important basic stroke, and no less important is the need to hit accurate cross-court shots. The initiative in any rally can quickly be lost by loose cross-court play. Not only will initiative be lost, but it will very often take you from attack to defence at a stroke. It is also true that players hit cross-court from the front too frequently, taking up the wrong option. It is a shot that is easy to play, especially under any sort of pressure. It also precludes too much thought, and so if you are not playing with awareness, at least be aware of the need to hit it in the right direction! It should be aimed to make contact with the side wall 30–45cm/12–18in behind the service box, struck low. Any shot short of this line, hitting the side wall early, or not wide enough, through the middle of the court, is a disaster.

The front-wall player should give himself room to play, moving in and out a little to prevent getting too close to the ball. He should also ensure that he is not playing behind his feet. The back player must also be continually adjusting his feet to give himself the best chance of assuming the most advantageous position.

Players are likely to thrive if they are both hitting the ball accurately, so do not let your partner down.

Common faults and weaknesses

Cross-court lob and angle, sometimes volleyed

An easy development from the previous practice is for the front player to lob cross-court instead of hitting low. The same positions need to be assumed and the lobber must aim for height, width and no pace. Players who have difficulty with the lob tend to hit it too hard or do not attain sufficient height because they fail to open the racket face.

When the front player is lobbing, the back-court player will often be in a position to volley the angle, especially if the lob is on target. The volleyed angle from deep in the court is no easy proposition and causes considerable difficulty on the forehand side. Although it is a shot that you will only employ from time to time, it has its value. Practising it also enhances racket skills, regardless of its more practical application.

The volleyed angle can sometimes be played to effect off the service and when cutting the ball off, further forward in the court on the mid-court line. Angles are effective, remember, against slow turners, moderate watchers and players coming under physical pressure.

Two drop shots

The first practice combined hitting straight with a drop shot from deep in the court, but drop shots are more commonly played at the front of the court, when there is more chance that your opponent is behind you. Players who lack a drop shot and consistently hit the ball deep are unable to take advantage of these situations. Practice will help to give you the necessary confidence to play the drop shot at appropriate times.

Practising two drop shots, one at the front of the court and one from a deeper position, requires one player to feed and one to play. The front player acts as the feeder, setting up a short ball followed by a ball lobbed into the service box. The ball at the front should be high enough to give the player the chance to make a good drop shot; the lobbed ball should be high enough to enable the player to move back, re-position, and play a satisfactory shot.

If the feeding is done accurately, the player will not only be able to play his shots well, but he will be able to establish a rhythm of movement that is sufficiently taxing without detracting from the object of the practice, which is to produce two accurate shots. Players should, of course, reverse roles. Practise down both sides, paying careful attention to correct footwork and racket production.

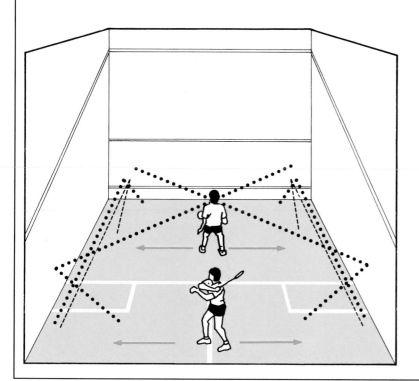

Straight hit combined with angle and drop

This is a variation on the previous practice of hitting straight with angle and movement.

To make the practice more testing for both players, the player in the back of the court has the added option of a drop shot, as well as the angle. This will give him a limited selection of shot, whereas the front player will be under more pressure of movement and will have to watch closely to determine his partner's intentions.

The difficulty of the practice can be further increased by allowing the front player to add the lob to his straight hit. The correct time to play the lob is not always easy to assess, so that will be at issue here.

Common faults and weaknesses

Cross-court lob with straight return followed by angle

This is by no means a simple practice since to return straight off an accurate lob is no easy matter. The front player will lob cross-court, high and wide, off which the back player has to play straight down the wall, keeping the ball as close to the wall as possible. The height at which the ball hits the front wall is immaterial – indeed, it will be valuable if the shot is played at varying heights.

The back player, of course, does not play the ball in short in this practice, though this has its value. The angle played off the straight return, has, as one of its objects, to bring the ball back to the lobber so that the practice may be maintained.

Although the straight return is more important than the angle, it is also important to play the angle as well as possible. This will necessitate a significant adjustment of the feet; whereas the straight return is best played sideways to the front wall, the angle requires a position facing the side wall in the direction in which the ball is to be struck.

When playing the straight return the player will be much closer to the side wall than he should be for the angle, where he will need to stand off both the side wall and the ball.

Two cross-courts, off fed balls, down one side of the court

This is another practice that requires one player to feed while the other plays.

The player works to the front of the court, then to a position at the back of the service box. From both positions he is required to play accurate cross-court shots which are low and wide so as to reach the side wall 30–45cm/12–18in behind the service box. So that the movement is not too pressurized, the feed will have to be sympathetically carried out, allowing the player time to get into favourable positions.

Both feeds should be set up quite lightly: the one to the front so that the player is not playing behind his feet; the one to the back should be given height on the front wall so as to allow the player time. The deeper shot is more difficult to play, since it is not so easy to hit the ball downwards from that position.

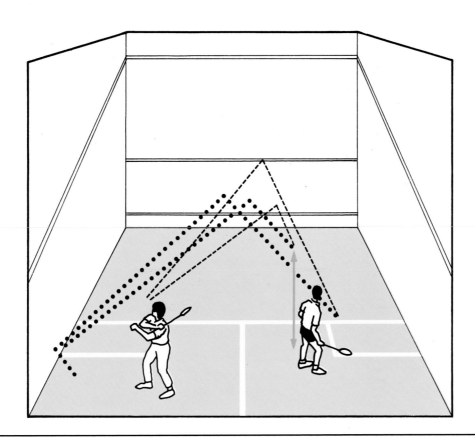

Chapter 4 IMPROVING YOUR GAME

Squash is essentially a competitive sport. Once you are confident that you have mastered the basic strokes and can play them well, you will soon realize the beneficial aspects of competition. Competitive matchplay at all levels is a means of sharpening your skills and gaining an insight into the whole new world of tactics and strategy, *temperament and mental agility. This chapter summarizes the needs of four distinct categories of player in order to illustrate how to progress through the competitive structure of the sport. Crucial to the development of any player is the advice and support of a good coach, and his role, both on and off court, is examined in detail.*

The ladder of success

The early part of this book has given you a basic armoury with which to tackle the competitive opportunities that the sport and its clubs can offer. The transition from the practice aspects of the basics to practical and competitive play is the next phase. It should reveal the degree of mastery of the basic skills that you have acquired. Self-induced pressure in the form of your desire to win immediately complicates the fundamental lessons you have learned. Opponents will constantly be attempting to play each stroke to the most difficult areas of the court i.e. the four corners, thereby making even the most elementary skills more difficult. This is the great challenge of the game of squash and is where even the beginner can derive the most fun.

The basic skills of squash are the foundation on which all players must build their competitive matchplay. Even at the higher levels, however, weaknesses will often be present, only exposed by more efficient or more skilful opponents. Thus, the

practices outlined in previous chapters must still be employed to continue reinforcing the correctness of disciplines that give the player every chance of competing at an increasingly high level of tournament play. For the purposes of investigating further the playing scale of improvement, playing standards have been loosely divided into four categories: players new to competitive play; club players; regular tournament players; and professional players.

Players new to competitive play

This type of player will have strong survival instincts and his tactical play will revolve around avoidance of errors both forced and, in particular, unforced. He will have assessed very rapidly that the requirement in a rally is merely to return the ball to the front wall one more time than his opponent and thus the necessary will have been achieved. He will have learnt to win a rally. Firstly, the serve will have been won and, pursuant to that, points will

At the beginning, mere physical survival can be interpreted as success. Improved fitness leads enticingly to the more skilful departments of the game

Finalists in an InterCity Pullman championship, a national competition for superior club players, gain their chance on the all-transparent showcourts usually reserved for top professionals

be acquired at the successful completion of each rally. This player tends to rely on physical assets to scurry around the court, generally retrieving his opponent's strokes with no great accuracy or direction, banking on the opposition making an error at the termination of what will frequently be a lengthy rally.

The player in this first category will gain confidence from being able to sustain lengthy rallies and will delight in his improving physical condition. Eventually, he will develop the desire to experiment with elementary stroke-making possibilities and the first impressions of tactical play, adding these to his solid foundations.

At this stage of development, the opportunity to gain experience and expertise is crucial and, therefore, the role of a coach or the chance to play better players should never be overlooked. The important adage at this point is: the longer the player can survive on court with a better player, the more he will learn. This puts a premium on the player being good at retrieving and being capable of hitting the ball safely and adequately into the back corners. He will have established the basic defensive game.

The player in this category will ideally be the member of a club league or ladder and will be progressing to the higher echelons of the club, rising ultimately to the possibilities of club team representative level in local leagues.

Club players
The club player is the culmination of category one. He has made the team

for local leagues, maybe not the first team, which will remain a major objective, but one of the lower divisions. In most team leagues, this will involve a whole season of programmed matches around which this category of player must evolve a system of practice matches and training to make the necessary preparation for optimum performance in critical encounters.

Physical, retrieving and defensive skills will still form the lion's share of this player's armoury, but the need to develop a more tactical approach than 'hit-and-run' will hasten the need to introduce something of a short game to the already overworked but effective hitting to the back corners. The emphasis will largely be on the latter and the short game will revolve around surprise winners or placements low over the tin that bounce close to the front wall – these are designed in particular to deprive the opponent of sufficient time to return the ball. A similar ploy can be achieved by increasing the accuracy and frequency in a rally of the use of the volley stroke. The volley must be

hit low over the tin and with a downward motion driven to fade second bounce into the back corners. This is a positive gesture of attack which will be the focus of great attention in work with the coach, who will be looking to build more incisive skills into his player's repertoire.

The more varied the styles of his opponents, the better opportunity the pupil will have to acquire the experience of different tactical ploys. He will assimilate, from his opponents' skills, a blend of tricks that are best suited to his own talents and develop a squash-playing style that expresses his own personality. This is a richly formative period of the player's development. With sound physical resources the player is equipped to cope with a heavy playing programme, and the learning process can accelerate quite quickly.

Regular tournament players
The regular tournament player is normally playing in the club's first team in the local league as well as in local tournaments. By now there is quite a compact and competitive player

The ladder of success

emerging with a good working knowledge of the game. His tactical ploys tend to be built around his attacking skills and on his ability to make winners, which is a difficult art, or on the construction of rallies using strokes designed to outmanoeuvre his opponent – or on both.

The degree of physical prowess at this level of play is still a vital ingredient as the strokes have increased in accuracy. A high degree of athleticism is therefore needed to maintain participation in the rallies, using prolonged defensive striking. However, physical assets are no longer the player's main tactical weapon. The dividing line between this category and the final top-flight professional is slim, but can be defined very loosely in terms of the player in the final category being able to beat his coach.

The regular tournament player will have gained a notable measure of success and will have experienced the practical usage of the basic strokes not only in local leagues but also in local area and regional individual tournaments. It is this category of player that gives British squash its tremendous depth of standard; Britain represents one of the top squash-playing nations in the world. There is also available to players in this category a large diversity of tournaments to satisfy the participants' competitive requirements.

Professional players
The professional player represents the ultimate development of the playing and physical skills of squash. The process will inevitably have started at a young age and progress to success

will have been unavoidably dramatic. This category of player is in the minority. Squash is not a wealthy sport and does not support the financial careers of many players – clearly there will be few who are good enough to succeed. This does not stop a large number of young players starting out on the adventure, but equally many fall by the wayside. To this end, it is important that the aspirant takes good advice at an early stage from a respected coach or manager, who will appraise and evaluate his long-term playing future as well as the possibilities when those days are numbered.

Advisors and mentors are just as invaluable to the professional player as they are to the novice. The most obvious example is the degree of success to which Jonah Barrington has al-

ways been able to motivate English team members at World Championships – it has always remained a mystery why his appointment has tended to be part-time rather than permanent.

The tactical approach at this level has to be flexible and varied to suit the nature of gaining the required result over the opposition. The player must therefore have a mastery over different styles of play. He must also have highly trained physical resources that can cope with the difficult combined demands of speed, agility, stamina and composure to succeed under the

Young players sneak their own moment on the showcourt between matches in the Spanish Open at the Castellana Squash Club in Madrid

Liz Irving (below left), top Australian
and one of the game's most inventive
stroke players, was on court from
childhood. Angela Smith (below)
encourages Yorkshire's Suzanne
Horner during a National
Championships quarter-final

severest of pressures inflicted by his
opponent. His racket work must
ideally encompass the hardest-
hitting attacking onslaught as well as
the deftest of touches for drop shots
and lobs, matched by basic stroking to
the back corners for defensive or
counter-attacking work. The combination of all these attributes helps
the player turn basic strokeplay into
effective matchplay.

This loose categorization is intended
as a working model of a player's
career development; it is by no means
definitive as there are many persona-
lities in squash who bring their own
brand of colour to the sport through
their play. Each player may bring his
own natural strengths to different
aspects of the game which will develop his competitive options from a
different tactical standpoint. For example, a highly-skilled racket player
may never come to depend on as high
a level of physical prowess as the
player who literally starts from
scratch with his basic strokes.
However, to progress to category
three and beyond the player must be
capable of combining successfully
the necessary areas of the game —
basic racket skills, physical prowess,
tactical skills and temperament — to
the required level of competence.

*Bryce Taylor works with Susan
Devoy (right) with whom he perfected
the game which dominates women's
competition. Rodney Martin (far
right), the finest product yet of the
Australian Institute of Squash, where
natural skills and talents are honed
to perfection*

The role of the coach

In most countries there is usually a reasonable competitive season of events that should offer players of all levels the opportunity to be active in the sport. Such is the challenge to improve that this should also provide a great source of fun. In charting the progress of the player through the categories mentioned previously, the coach enjoys a special role that should be looked at in more detail.

The coach can make the passage up the ladder an educated and safe one, and hopefully relatively speedy. The nature of squash is such that the 'hit-and-run' players, or those of 'brute force and ignorance', can do reasonably well with a degree of perseverance and determination. Ultimately, however, such progress will grind to a halt as the self-taught player will be relatively limited in his approach. Coached players, who learn the more skilful methods, will cope with the ferocious but largely inaccurate hitting and manoeuvre him to defeat. However, suffice it to say that 'hit-and-run' can go a long way by simply increasing the efficiency of the methods, and it is only in recent times that it has been necessary to add a full range of accurate strokes to a sound defensive base in order to reach the highest levels. Learning the offensive skills demands the assistance of a coach who can teach good technique and, more importantly, the correct usage of attacking strokes to ensure maximum return.

Safety and etiquette
The safety aspect is one that should not be overlooked, as on the squash court both contestants are on the 'same side of the net' and are in close proximity. The squash racket is potentially a lethal weapon, as is a squash ball, and there are certain elementary courtesies aimed to ensure that a player is never short of opponents because of anti-social play. For example, it is a point scored if a player hits the ball and strikes his opponent with it on the way to the front wall. However, should this happen more than once in anything more than an accident, the match may well deteriorate rapidly. Similarly, the receiver of service is not expected 'to turn on the ball' in the backhand corner and strike the ball forehand (or vice versa) to an area where his opponent is most likely to be positioned, thus endangering life and limb of the server. Such courtesies are necessary for maximum enjoyment of the game and a let or the replay of the rally will ensure that your matches pass off uneventfully.

Advice and encouragement
The coach is normally seen as a teacher of the basics, including etiquette, to the beginner, but a good coach will run courses for all levels of the club's players, including juniors. Frequently he will assist with the training of the club's teams and watch, encourage and motivate them. He may even lead from the front in the first team.

The coach must be good at analysing matchplay and supply words of

Rahmat Khan, the man behind the training and practice techniques that led a 17-year-old Jahangir to a 5½-year undefeated reign

wisdom in the minute gaps between games. These need not be highly technical but do need to encourage and motivate the pupil to greater endeavours. This role becomes increasingly important for the coach as his pupil rises to the highest levels and spends less time on court with him. The coach can and should, even then, play the part of feeder in practice sessions. The coach must keep vigilant for technical faults that appear in his player's game and look to rectify them before these problems escalate into loss of confidence and bad form. Such observation can lead to isolating frequent areas of error and, therefore, give rise to some hard work to rectify the problem.

An obvious source of error is in the player's work at the front of the court, because the strokes will be played so close to the tin. It is here that minor adjustments can be made to raise the

ball from out of the tin into the inch-perfect winner. The drop shot, with the added difficulty of judging the right amount of touch to apply to the stroke, is perhaps the biggest single problem that many players face. However, once it is mastered it can be the most damaging weapon to use against an opponent – if it does not win the point outright it can frequently exert a high drain on his energy resources since it requires a violent lunge to make good the return of just such a successful 'dink'.

Match manager

The coach should have a high level of squash expertise to assist in the pupil's development on the court and this is clearly the vital ingredient, but there is another role that is sometimes undertaken by the coach – that of match manager. This role involves planning a season's matches, i.e. tournaments that are to be played and the league teams in which the player will compete. Such arrangements encompass travel details, accommodation, the timing of matches, meals before and after the event, some press coverage for publicity purposes, some sponsorship (even if this amounts only to free sponsors' T-shirts) and any activities that lead to successful results.

This may seem to be the domain of only the top players in the sport but players at all levels should benefit from attention to the smooth-running of their playing activities. A player who competed once a week was frequently known to take that day off work to make sure of obtaining the best possible result, and it was a sur-

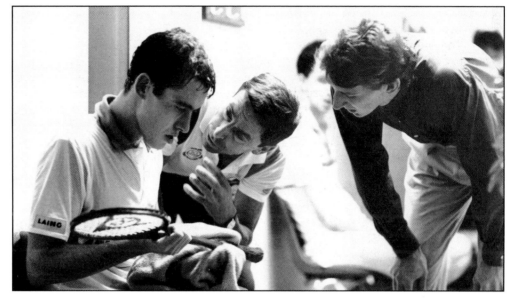

Jonah Barrington, the first and ultimate pro in squash, sends Bryan Beeson back on court in the 1987 World Open Championships ready to fight to the death for success. Gawain Briars looks on in quiet admiration

prise to learn that he did not find it necessary to take the following day off as well bearing in mind the exposure that he managed to obtain for his result, be it good or bad! It is not to be recommended on a frequent basis if full-time employment is involved!

The top professionals may deem it necessary to take on board managerial experts, but the simple administrative problems of running league teams for clubs usually fall to the most dedicated enthusiasts who work voluntarily for the good of the team. The task on a mundane level is a daunting one and can be hair-raising when trying to obtain match fees from team players and ensuring that players all arrive for the match on time – some may say this is a full-time occupation! Such organizers are the life-blood of squash and provide the opportunity for so many to enjoy the game. The selection and marshalling of a team can be a nightmare, by the

time a squad of players has been systematically reduced with the unavailability of the best players, lost to a prestige event being held on the same date, and others due to injury. These problems are relatively commonplace and arise at all standards of competition.

Any success obtained by a team is generated by good team spirit, a large squad of players, and the right standard of players with the determination to succeed, but most importantly by a good team manager. It has been said that squash is an individual sport and that players should be self-sufficient, because in the hour of need a player has to be a winner and has only his own resources to rely on. However, the course of many a match has been changed by organizational skills or coaching expertise. There is sometimes no need of great technical advice – a friendly face to encourage is usually quite sufficient.

Match report **THE KILLER INSTINCT**

Event: Thorntons ISPA
Championship Final
Venue: Abbeydale Park, Sheffield,
UK
Date: 10 March, 1982
Scoreline: Jahangir Khan (Pakistan)
bt Maqsood Ahmed (Pakistan)
9–0 9–0 9–0

'The greatest exhibition of concentrated squash I have ever seen,' was how Jonah Barrington summed up Jahangir Khan's demolition of Maqsood Ahmed in the final of the International Squash Players Association Championship at Abbeydale Park, Sheffield, on 10 March, 1982.

On this occasion the great man certainly could not be accused of overstatement. The highly knowledgeable Yorkshire gallery had just been treated to a truly remarkable spectacle, the like of which had not been witnessed anywhere for over fifty years. Jahangir Khan had beaten Maqsood Ahmed without conceding a point – the first time the feat had been achieved in a major men's final since 1931. Nor indeed has it happened again since.

The Abbeydale annihilation lasted a mere 24 minutes, during which Maqsood Ahmed won just six rallies. He did not play at all badly, particularly in the first two games. However, he found himself hopelessly outclassed by an opponent whose movement, racket work and reading of the game on the night reached a combined peak above which it was impossible to imagine any player ascending.

Of course those facets of Jahangir Khan's game had always been impressive. Ever since defeating Phil Kenyon in the world amateur final at Melbourne in September 1979 at the age of fifteen, Jahangir Khan had displayed the qualities of a champion in ever increasing depth with every appearance on court. It was obvious

that the young man was going to be something very special when he fought out the heart-stopping 1981 British Open Final with Geoff Hunt before eventually losing after two hours and 13 minutes. He fulfilled that promise when he ended the Australian's five-year reign as world champion in Toronto six months later.

But another six months on in Sheffield it became clear that Jahangir Khan possessed in abundance yet another quality and one that is gifted only to the really extraordinary performers in any sphere. Jahangir Khan displayed in no uncertain terms against Maqsood Ahmed that he had within his psychological make-up a well-defined streak of ruthlessness – the 'killer instinct' that identifies the truly great champions in the history of competitive sport.

The eighteen-year-old collected his nine points of the opening game in one hand and repeated the exercise in the third – remarkable statistics against a man six years his senior and ranked fourth in the world. Even more remarkable against a fellow countryman who, as one of Pakistan's finest players of recent years, will certainly have been numbered among his heroes during the early years of his life. Add the fact that the gallery spent most of the match vociferously willing Maqsood Ahmed to register a point, and the degree of Jahangir Khan's ruthlessness becomes even more apparent.

'At what stage in the match did

*Jahangir, the cool young executioner;
Maqsood, the experienced,
unbelieving master*

Jahangir decide to go for the white-wash?' queried one member of the squash press after the match. 'Was it as early as the flashing backhand cross-court winner that took the score in the opening game to 8−0 or as late as when a replica of that shot edged him to 4−0 in the third?' Incidentally, it was from that point onwards that Jahangir Khan had to withstand a completely different type of pressure as, for the first time in the match, the Abbeydale spectators switched their allegiance to him, willing him to retain the clean sheet about which they could talk from first-hand knowledge to their grandchildren.

There was never a conscious decision taken to try for a 27−0 win, according to Jahangir Khan. 'When I am playing a match, I am always aiming to win each individual point. I never seriously think about winning 27−0, but against Maqsood everything I did worked. It was just one of those matches.' To accept that modest assessment would be to undervalue grossly a superb athletic performance. It would also greatly underestimate the detailed pre-match preparation and, perhaps most significantly, would fail to give credit to the utterly ruthless manner in which Jahangir Khan carried the results of that preparation on to the court and through the match.

The youngster started the final at a cracking pace, volleying everything he could early and powerfully. Maqsood Ahmed had survived a particularly strenuous semi-final, beating Gawain Briars 9−7 in the fifth, while Jahangir Khan had cruised past Gamal Awad for the loss of six points. The

Renowned for his front-court delicacy, Maqsood Ahmed was deprived of any kind of rhythm under relentless pressure

older man was bound to be feeling the more tired, and his young compatriot wasted no time in exposing that weakness.

By the end of the opening game, Maqsood Ahmed had been physically battered and mentally assaulted. And there was no let-up in the second, with Jahangir Khan keeping up the relentless pressure by mixing the stretching volleys with a variety of cruel short drops and boasts. Maqsood Ahmed was not allowed to settle into any kind of rhythm nor to become involved in the exchanges of front-court delicacy for which he was renowned. As they left the court, he looked a broken man. He had not played badly but had still to score a point.

It was difficult not to feel sympathy for Maqsood Ahmed during the third game, as he struggled between the conflicting desires of attempting to put his name on the scoresheet and retreating as swiftly as possible from the scene of such an embarrassing reversal. Jahangir Khan obviously felt

At what stage did Jahangir opt for the whitewash? Was it when the Abbeydale spectators began to urge him to the clean sheet?

no such sympathy. He proceeded about his task without any sign of emotion and completed his perfect score against a thoroughly dispirited opponent.

Even after registering the twenty-seventh point to tumultuous applause from the gallery, only the merest hint of a smile was permitted to cross the face of the teenage world champion. His first thought was for his vanquished compatriot who was the recipient of a warm handshake and an almost apologetic shake of the head. It was a friendly gesture which may somehow have eased the pain of Maqsood Ahmed's humiliation. But the abiding memory from that March evening in 1982 was the ruthlessness to which he had been subjected over the previous 24 minutes.

Toronto had hailed Jahangir Khan the champion. Now Sheffield heralded Jahangir Khan the destroyer. Killer instinct had been added to the already terrifying list of attributes possessed by the youngest world number one in the history of squash.

Chapter 5 THE MIND GAME

Squash, perhaps more than any other sport, calls upon a vast range of attributes. All of these – physical, technical, temperamental and tactical – are called into play at various times and in various degrees by the command centre. How well and how fully you use them depends on your mind game. Without the right commands the battle is disjointed, ineffective and inefficient. This chapter looks at the structure and rules you can use to help take command of these attributes and play winning squash.

The command centre

First, let us look at what attributes are required. In squash, the fittest survive and usually win. Fitness involves many things. Craig Sharp, Chief Physiologist at the British Olympic Medical Centre, says:

'What one might call "total Fitness" consists of excellence in perhaps six areas of body function: oxygen transport (heart, lungs and blood); muscle endurance; muscle speed; muscle strength; joint flexibility; and body composition. For the squash player, only strength is not required to any high degree, although there is a minimal requirement! These six fitness components are each capable of being altered by training, and each is capable of being assessed in the laboratory.'

'One of the excellent features of squash as a recreational sport is that it requires a wide variety of fitness qualities.'

Related to fitness, but in a category of its own, is movement. In 1987 Jansher Khan burst on to the international squash scene with a speed and fluidity of movement unmatched by any of his opponents. This ability over any other took him to the world championship title.

How fast someone moves can be seen in their ability to take off, stop in a balanced stance, recover, turn and change direction.

Squash is a game of skill as much as of stamina. How well a player hits the ball – the pace, accuracy, consistency, and variety of his shots – is crucial to his success. This incorporates technique, talent, practice and of course shot selection.

Temperamentally, squash is a tough combative sport. Players are locked together in close physical proximity in a battle that is mental as well as physical. The mental battle to assert yourself over an opponent is

also a battle with yourself to overcome nervousness, fear, irritation, expectations, to be disciplined, positive, determined and to concentrate without lapses.

Squash is sometimes referred to as a physical game of chess. The moves you make are crucial. Some players seem to make these moves totally at random and suffer the same fate as a chess player who plays with such an inclination. Behind the moves is the plan – the strategy or tactics. If this plan is vague, your game will lack clarity in direction and precision in its execution.

Squash is a rallying sport, not just a shot-making duel. The plan behind the 'moves' employed in a rally is crucial to a player's success. When players' physical and technical attributes are of a similar level the battle becomes mental and tactical. The best tactical player wins.

The command centre brings together all the ingredients in a player's game. How well each is fulfilled, and how well these ingredients are mixed, depends on the mind game. Most players are capable of improving their game just by re-ordering the things they do, i.e. by giving the right commands.

Mark Cairns, angry with a refereeing decision, throws down his racket and risks losing his concentration

Gawain Briars attends both to muscle fatigue and competitive planning in the short noisy break between games at the 1984 World Masters

Squash is a mental battle with your opponent and also with yourself. Aim to overcome and control nerves, to concentrate and to come up with a 'performance'.

A champion's temperament allows him to play near his best consistently, where for other players their performance can fluctuate. Outside pressures and worries must be blotted out. Attention should be narrowed purely to the game, but must still allow a player to pick up all cues.

Arousal must be high to allow a player to perform. Take time before a match to psych yourself up. This may initially involve relaxation, and then

Jansher Khan, unmatched for speed and fluidity of movement, plays a perfect wrong-footing backhand drop

psyching. Start to concentrate on the task ahead, and mentally rehearse strokes and tactics. Concentration is the key to a good mental performance. Much depends on your ability to think clearly and to keep on track.

As a player you will have experienced that dumbfounded confusion immediately after having tried to play two shots at the same time or of having changed your mind and shot at the last minute with poor results. Perhaps you attempt shots from poor

positions and end up playing tactically inept shots because you stick to an original idea of what you would ideally like to do, rather than adapting to the type of ball you have to work with. Do not make your game too complex. Keep it simple and keep your decisions simple.

Be aware of the danger areas where concentration can drift and lapse:

1 Do not relax after a good lead, especially on a match or game-ball. The match is not yet won.

2 Do not let your disappointment or anger affect your concentration after a mistake, tactical error, bad decision, or after losing a long rally.

3 Block out distractions like crowd noise, a break (e.g. a broken ball), opponents' distracting and delaying tactics, the non-arrival of support.

Squash requires instant decision making. You are in command of a large number of attributes and will need to use them to the full. Use simple rules and deviate from them only as an exception. Discipline yourself to use 'the plan' and the appropriate 'plays' and 'moves' in your rallies.

The plan

The final event in a squash rally is not necessarily the most significant. Dominance may have been established, or an opening prized, well before this. Events that result in points being won and lost add up to the key factors in winning and losing games.

Your plan focuses on these, and orders all the other events that occur in a rally, i.e. recovering the ball, defending, playing tight shots, hitting hard, using attacking shots, moving your opponent etc. It should provide a coherent framework that you can use to help make decisions and order priorities.

There are three main phases of play:

1 Defence The first and most crucial part of your game is defence. This involves court coverage, getting the ball safely back and not giving your opponent easy balls.

2 Pressure and positional play The second part of your game is about pressuring your opponent into making mistakes and creating openings to attack.

3 Attack As well as not losing points, you want to win them. You will use winners and passing shots.

These are three phases of play or 'plays' that you use in a game or rally. Having a plan helps determine which is the most appropriate at each stage of the game or rally.

Tactical balance

Tactics are about the balance between the various 'plays' you can use in a match – between defence and attack and between pressure and positional play. Start your match and each rally with defence. Wait for and force openings before you move on to the attack.

If defensive shots are loosely defined as back-quarter shots, and attacking shots as front-quarter shots, a suitable balance between the two may be seventy-five per cent defensive and twenty-five per cent attacking. Keep your game simple. Defence first, then pressure and positional play to create openings, and attack to finish.

Pace

The best tactical player controls the pace of the game. The pace of a shot governs the time you have to recover the 'T', and the time your opponent has to get to it. Obviously you will want to deprive your opponent of time, and will tend to want to hit hard, but this will also deprive you of time. When you are under pressure or tired, slow the game down

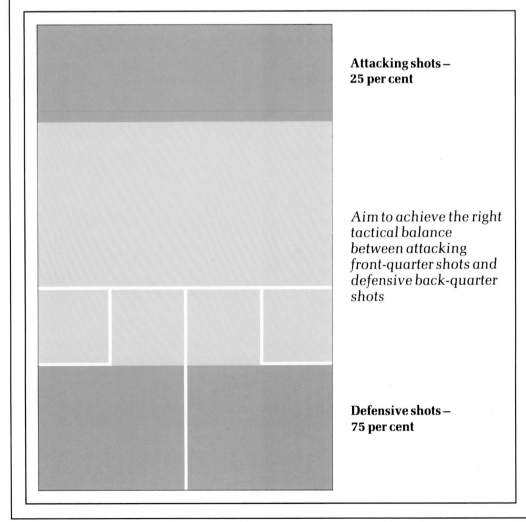

Attacking shots –
25 per cent

Aim to achieve the right tactical balance between attacking front-quarter shots and defensive back-quarter shots

Defensive shots –
75 per cent

Hiddy Jahan, possessor of the strongest and most deceptive forearm in the game, at full stretch to convert his opponent's attack into the top right corner by driving the ball deep down the forehand wall

with lobs and high balls. Play each shot, each rally, and the game at the pace you want.

Experiment a little to find the pace that works best for you with a particular opponent. Some players are dynamic at a fast pace, but lose all assertiveness if it is slow.

Strengths and weaknesses

Play the game to your strengths and your opponent's weaknesses. Set up the rallies you want and assert yourself. Look for the openings you want and fight with your opponent to control the rallies. Do this before worrying about winning points.

Plan the game to attack your opponent's weaknesses, physical, technical, tactical and mental. For example, if he is impatient, prolong the rallies; if he is tense, play fast and rush him; if he is slow, use surprise short shots; if he cannot volley; then lob; if he is unfit, move him. Adapt your plan, your play and your moves to work on an opponent's deficiencies.

Changing your game

The rules are very simple:

1 Do not change a winning game When you have the tactical balance right for your opponent, do not spoil it – you may not be able to get it back.

2 Change a losing game If you are playing loosely or are making errors or are pressurized, revert 'back to basics', i.e. more defence. If you are rallying comfortably but are not winning points you may need to plan more attacking shots or exert more pressure.

A change of pace, placement or type of shot can turn the tide. This is why you should try to develop a number of tactical possibilities in your practice games. You should have an alternative tactical option which you can try on your opponent as you search for weaknesses to attack.

Susan Devoy prepares to attack in the top backhand corner, having forced Lisa Opie to play a loose mid-court shot from the forehand court

The play

What are the key things you should be concentrating on in a rally and how should you go about them? Let us look at various types of play and when to use them.

Squash matches are won and lost on mistakes. Most of these are unnecessary. To keep the ball in play, the ball must be hit on the volley or first bounce. It must hit the front wall above the tin and below the out-of-court line. The front wall is 6.40m/21ft wide. Squash has the marvellous advantage that the other three walls can be used to angle the ball to the front. Unlike tennis, this makes passing shots difficult as a player has a second, and sometimes a third, occasion on which to hit a ball.

The front wall is big. All a player must be able to do is get the ball up on that wall. Often the propensity, i.e. impacts per area, with which the ball hits the tin is greater than that with which it hits the front wall itself. The tin is the main area where mistakes are made. Other mistakes are mishits (including misses, mistimed shots, woods, double hits and carried shots), shots that are down and those that are out.

How successful you are depends on how well you avoid these problems and get the ball back safely. What is required is quite simple. You need to get to the ball and get it up on the front wall without a mistake.

Getting to the ball
Getting to the ball, or more correctly getting in position to play the shot you want, is not just a matter of fitness. Fitness means sustaining this ability over a period of time. Court coverage involves basic habits that must be ingrained.

Always watch the ball and your opponent. Do not become a 'front wall watcher', and pick the ball up late, depriving yourself of vital time and hence risking a rushed shot or even not getting there at all. When

your opponent is about to hit the ball, look for clues as to its direction, by watching his footwork, position and backswing. Do not guess, but be ready to anticipate.

To get to every ball you will need to stand in the best position on court and be ready to move in every direction. The best position is called on the 'T', and this is about a racket length behind the intersection of the half and short lines.

The ready position is where your feet are on each side of the half-court line; your toes are to the front and you are crouched with your weight forwards over the balls of your feet. In this position you are ready to move instantly in any direction, unlike a sprinter in the blocks who is committed to moving in one direction.

Top players are usually found back in position, on the 'T', before their opponent has hit the ball. This is an ability they have developed and is one of the main reasons why they are at the top.

In a squash rally you can only stop twice – when you are hitting the ball and when you are back in position on the 'T'. It is easy to find excuses like 'I'm too tired', 'I was unlikely to get it anyway' or 'I was anticipating' (meaning guessing). It is also easy to stop and watch your opponent rather than moving and watching, but you must force yourself to get to the ball and then recover the 'T'.

Jahangir Khan, back on the 'T' even before his opponent reaches the ball

Del Harris, drawn into the deep court, slips when trying to recover, wrong-footed too far behind the 'T' by a disguised long drop shot from Rodney Martin

Here, mental strength as well as physical stamina is required. Discipline yourself and show how determined you are. Do not be put off, because success depends on your basic determination to get the ball back.

Avoiding mistakes

Mistakes are made in all areas of the game – technical, tactical, mental and physical. Mishits and mistakes can occur because of technical faults, tension or physical tiredness. However, the vast majority are avoidable and are made because you are not thinking clearly.

Although some nerves are useful, excessive nervousness affects the mind's capacity to think, to solve problems and to take in signals from the game. In a highly nervous state, therefore, your capacity to concentrate is weakened.

Nervousness is a cause of 'inexplicable' mistakes. These can be overcome by relaxation techniques, good match preparation, taking time in the knock-up, and using a defensive playing-in period which concentrates on safety and basic drives.

As well as the mental effects, excessive nervousness causes physical stress. The body reacts by tightening the muscles, resulting in less efficient movement. It also makes timing a shot difficult and results in misses, mishits and less accuracy.

Anxiety can strike at any time in a match and may result in an overeagerness to win points. If this happens, go back to a playing-in period.

Once on court, your span of attention needs to be narrowed to the task ahead. Upsets and worries at work and home, and all other distracting problems, need to be cleared out of the mind. When concentration goes, the rules and plan that you use to order your game drift away, and mistakes are easy to make.

In a game, give yourself checks and immediate aims when you stop to serve or receive. Practise your thinking on court.

When you examine a score sheet, you will notice that mistakes do not occur randomly but in groups and runs of points. These are lapses, i.e. a loss of concentration for a period, often resulting in a string of mistakes.

Lapses are particularly prevalent after a distracting or disappointing event. For example, you have made a mistake and lost a long rally; your opponent has hit a lucky shot; the referee has awarded a 'no-let' or a 'stroke' against you; you have slipped, been hit or suffered a collision; there is a dispute or an incident on court; your opponent wastes time; the ball breaks – these are all potential danger areas.

On the first mistake, tactical error or sign of a lapse, all the warning bells should be ringing and you should immediately pull your game together. Give yourself something to concentrate on each time you come to receive, even if it is just thinking, 'Do not make a mistake'.

Players hit the tin for one reason only – they aim too low. Of course they do not mean to hit the tin, they do not aim into it, they just do not aim high enough. High enough, that is, to allow for a margin of error. How high you aim above the tin will depend on how accurate you are, how difficult the ball is that you are attacking, and your opponent's position. Aim high enough so as to avoid mistakes.

Allow for a margin of error on all shots. It is better to aim a little lower on the out-of-court line at the side, for the service and lob, than to risk hitting out. It is better to hit a little longer than shorter and risk an easy ball being attacked.

Wait for and force out easy balls to attack. A high percentage of mistakes are made because often difficult balls are chosen to attack. This may be cause of poor decision making, inadequate understanding of tactical

The play

rules or impulsiveness and lack of discipline. Do not take risks with difficult balls. Wait for an easy one and minimize the risk.

Defending

Squash is a defensive game: the player with the best defensive game usually wins. The first battle in squash is for control of the 'T'. The 'T', or centre position, is the strategic ground that is being fought over. You win the 'T' by getting your opponent out of position and into the back corners. Usually, your opponent will fight back and possession of the 'T' will fluctuate. The player who gains the most possession will dominate the rallies.

The defensive part of your game is based on shots of good width and length. Good-length shots, which hit the floor behind the service box, the back, and then rebound, will force your opponent right into the corners. Your opponent will have to wait for the ball to come off and fall, thereby giving you time to recover the 'T'.

Good width is where the ball is angled into the side wall to beat the volley. However, it should not rebound enough to provide an easy ball. On a cross-court drive the target area is usually the side wall behind the service box.

The key factor in defence is to eliminate weak shots and deprive your opponent of the opportunity of winning points. To do this, use the principles of length and width for placement, and vary the pace of your shots, to give time when you need it.

Technically, you have a range of swings from a full swing to a short push. The shorter the swing, the easier the preparation, the steadier the stance through impact, the more care and deliberation taken on the shot, the more accurate and safe it will be. At times you will be under pressure, off balance, stretched, twisted and poorly placed for a shot. You should not in these circumstances attempt a full swing.

Co-ordination of movement between moving player, racket and ball is a complex operation. As you move in and prepare to hit you are faced not only with the decision of where to hit the ball, but how to hit it. Occasionally it will be easier and safer to use a compact or short swing and lift the ball a little higher and wider. You will see players who cannot or will not adapt their technique, and attempt to play every shot full out, resulting in some inaccuracy and hence weak, or 'loose' shots.

Try to eliminate casual, as well as weak shots from your game. Prepare and line up each shot. Work into the best position. Top players play their best shots nearly all the time, but they have to work at it.

The first part of your game is defensive. Do not be in a hurry to change this. When the opening presents itself, attack. Have confidence in your plan and do not be distracted by isolated events, or attempt lucky shots. Play to a pattern and maintain discipline. Be patient and wait for the openings; try to force weak balls by playing your best shots.

Get the defensive part of your game working at the start of each rally. Win control of the 'T', put your opponent out of position in the back and deprive him of opportunities.

Creating openings

Beginners see the coup de grâce of a squash rally as the key to winning and losing. Dominance, however, may have been established well before this or the opening may have been surrendered, forced or prized out over a number of shots.

The first phase of play is often defensive; as soon as this is established you should look for and try to create openings to attack. There are three ways of creating openings in squash: the tight defensive game, forcing weak balls; the pressure game, depriving your opponent of time; and the positional game, where you manoeuvre your opponent out of position and then play the ball away from him.

The pressure game

Squash is a pressure game. Aim to deprive your opponent of time, so that he does not get to the ball in time to hit it; pressurize him into making mistakes; have him scraping the ball up so that he plays weak shots you can finish off. You can do this by taking the ball early on the bounce, by volleying and by hitting hard.

Obviously, the sooner you hit the ball the less time your opponent has to get back into position. The harder you hit the ball the faster it goes; it is more difficult to get at and gives your opponent less time in which to swing. Volleying may cut the time down for your opponent to recover the 'T' by at least a half. The great Geoff Hunt, eight times winner of the British Open, based much of his game on the volley. Search out the volleys in your game. Fight for the 'T' and hang on to it by volleying. Volley to keep your opponent in the back.

Too often, there is a far higher percentage of errors on the volley than on other shots, because players feel that everything should be attacked. This is wrong. As with your ground strokes, pick the balls to attack and allow a margin of error. On the volley you have a full range of shots. Each should be mastered and worked into your game.

Restrict your opponent with your defensive game. Study his returns and patterns of play and anticipate his responses without over-committing yourself.

Aim your drives to cling to the side wall in the back corner. If a cross-court is not possible and you can cover the boast, move in to cut off his return with a volley drop or volley boast. If his return is difficult, volley cross-court or for a straight length. If it is tight you may have to give up the 'T' and wait for another opportunity. Squash is also a waiting game.

Set up the moves. If your opponent is at the back, look to volley short. Push your opponent to the front and then intercept his return and smash it away to a dying length. Wait for the loose cross-court and cut it off on the volley. Play a drop so tight that he can only go down the wall and then move in and volley deep.

When you play a volley, it is unlikely that your opponent will be back in position. You are depriving him of time and this pressure can force a weak shot. These are the openings you desire. To attack without an opening is often suicidal.

A squash ball slows down considerably over its bounce and especially when it is rebounding off a wall. You deprive your opponent of time by taking it early on the bounce and before it reaches the side or the back. When your opponent is back, consider boasting a ball that is a little

Del Harris, young but a past master at converting defence to attack through his unorthodox racket work

shorter than a full length, rather than giving your opponent the extra time by waiting for it to come off the back.

If you can, drive a ball on the rise, before it gets to the side. Fit in the opportunist half-volley when the positions are to your advantage.

Tactics are a balance between attack and defence, and hard and soft shots. Do not sacrifice control and just bash a ball around the court; vary the pace and give yourself time. However, having said this, the player who hits the ball hardest and longest is often the winner. The harder the ball is hit, the faster it travels, the less time an opponent has to get to it and the more difficult it is to hit. Hit hard. Do not give your opponent time to recover, get in and knock him off court.

There is a big difference between depriving your opponent and depriving yourself of time. If you are out of position, or under pressure, give yourself the time you need. If your opponent is out of position, tired, rushing or anxious, turn the pressure on him. If you are applying pressure by hitting hard, this will take more out of you physically, so remember to

The play

pace yourself through the match.

Deprive your opponent of time by applying pressure through volleying, taking the ball early and hitting hard. Force mistakes and force out weak balls that you can attack or smash away as passing shots.

The positional game
Squash is a positional game. It is quite possible that, when two players of similar skills walk on the court, one will leave tired and defeated, although his shots are as good as his opponent's and he is as fit. He has been forced to work harder than his opponent; forced out of position and then moved over a distance. One player has asserted himself tactically.

Squash is a battle over territory. You use shots, various paces of shot and angles to outmanoeuvre your opponent. The important thing is not how good your shots are, but how well you select them. The mind game is about playing the right shot at the right time.

The basic rule for the positional game is fairly simple and sums up what you are trying to do in squash: hit the ball away from your opponent.

This is obvious, you may say, but it is not something that is generally observed when watching squash. When you are under pressure, running, hitting, recovering, it is not so easy to calculate an opponent's position, the openings and the best response to each situation. Too often we make our decisions unnecessarily complex. Do not confuse good tactical sense by trying to wrong-foot your opponent, use deception or by endeavouring to wear him out.

Keep it simple. When deciding what to do with a ball, there are two main considerations. Firstly, play it safely. Secondly, play it away from your opponent. Here we come back to our key tactical problem – getting the right balance between defence and attack. You are not trying to move your opponent on every ball. Play safely, but when you have an opportunity to move him, take it. Move into your positional game.

It is so easy when you are watching a match from the gallery to see the tactical mistakes others make. A player has his opponent trapped out of position on one side of the court and hits the ball cross-court straight back to him. From the back, the ball has been

1 The player in the back corner has played a loose straight drive, creating an attacking opportunity for the striker.

2 The striker pounces on this opportunity with a volley boast.

3 This combination moves his opponent on the diagonal. This is the furthest he can make him run in a straight line.

hit loose and short with the player stuck behind the striker, who rushes in and hits it straight to the back. One of the main tactical errors in squash is to play short when your opponent is in the front court, or on the 'T', i.e. when he is in the best possible position to retrieve it.

You may sometimes be confused by the alternatives open to you. Of course, you should approach your shots with various options in mind, perhaps disguising them, but try to keep your decisions simple. Variation, deception and wrong-footing an opponent are exceptions to the general rule. Take your opportunities to hit the ball away from your opponent and hit it as far away as possible.

Follow these simple positional rules:

---

1 Do not play short when your opponent is in the front or on the 'T'.
2 Get your opponent out of position in the back of the court and, when you have the opening, move him to the front.
3 Play short when your opponent is behind you.
4 Only rally short if you can cover all your opponent's alternatives.
5 Hit the ball as far away from your opponent as possible.
6 Do not hit the ball back to your opponent.
7 Move your opponent up and down the court.
8 Put your opponent to the front and follow up with a volley.

Defence is an important part of your game, but if it is only defence, it is hard work and negative. The openings must be forced out and used. To apply pressure and create openings, move your opponent and keep moving him. The cumulative effect of several shots, where your opponent is running for a ball and even further out of position, can give you the opening to finish off the rally.

Do not just push in isolated shots to move an opponent, but follow up with a volley, or a pressure shot. Perhaps an opponent's options have been narrowed, by a clinging drop or drive, allowing you to anticipate his next move. Many top professionals put their opponents short and stand right up on the 'T' looking for the chance to intercept.

Winning points

There is both joy and satisfaction to be gained from playing winning shots. This can be dangerous. It is dangerous because squash is a percentage game. As mentioned earlier, most matches are won and lost on mistakes. It is not how good your winning shots are that is important, but how good you are at calculating when to play them.

Going for too many winners and hence making mistakes and tactical errors, i.e. providing openings for your opponent, is only one side of the problem. The other is not going for winners.

Squash is not an ascetic or physical exercise. It is competition. It involves anxiety, stress and fear. Anxiety can hinder receiving clear signals on the openings, and can affect the decision-making process. Physical stress or tension make playing precise winners difficult. Fear of losing or making mistakes leads to a nervous retreat into defensive and negative play. These are, of course, problems that the competitor must overcome.

The most useful tool for overcoming overexuberance or fear about going for winners is a very clear understanding of when they should be played. There are two main danger areas when playing a winning shot: firstly, you may hit the tin and, secondly, your opponent may get the ball and smash it away to finish the rally. The first is solved, to some extent, by picking the best possible conditions. You need an easy ball and time to play it. How often have you stabbed at a ball:— clinging to the wall; angled sharply into the side; almost out of reach on the volley or skidding across the floor and then played a poor shot into the tin? You also need some positional advantage that allows you to aim high enough above the tin, to have a suitable margin of error.

The second problem is solved by picking a time to attack when your opponent is out of position. The problem with attacking when your opponent is in position is that you provide an opening that he can exploit, and you may well not be able to cover his range of potential shots, i.e. you can be caught out of position. It is time to attack when:

1 You have an easy ball.
2 Your opponent is out of position.

Generally, we refer to the front-court game as the attacking game, but often these moves will throw up a weak ball that should be volleyed or driven to die in the back, or killed cross-court away from an opponent.

The moves

Squash, like chess, is made up of moves and counter-moves. These involve instant decision making as there is little time for delibera-tion. Many of the moves made will be standard. Alternatives and varia-tions, however, will be used so that the game is not predictable.

1 The striker turns and moves towards the back corner while his opponent moves to recover position on the 'T'.

2 The striker positions himself to the side of the ball and waits for it to come off the back between him and the side wall so that he can play a straight drive.

3 The striker has swung under the ball and endeavoured to lift it straight and high on to the front wall.

4 The player on the 'T' prepares to move into the back cor-ner to return the ball. This sequence is used in the circling pairs practice exercise.

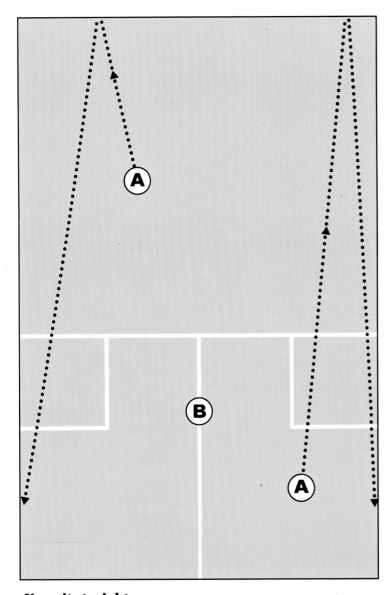

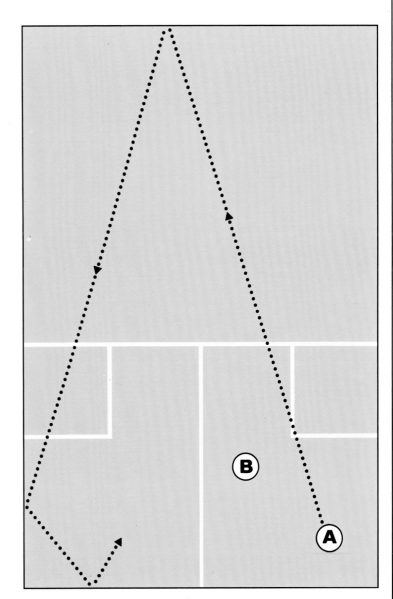

Keep it straight

Defence is the basis of your plan. It provides a stable base or pattern to your play. The most basic thing you can do is hit straight. Keep your game mainly straight and vary it from there. The straight shot is the standard return of serve.

Look for opportunities to cross-court

The cross-court is an excellent shot because it does not bounce out from the back as much as a straight drive and can therefore force boasts and weak returns. Play a cross-court when your opponent is out of position on one side, or back off the 'T', where the width of your shot will beat his volley.

The moves

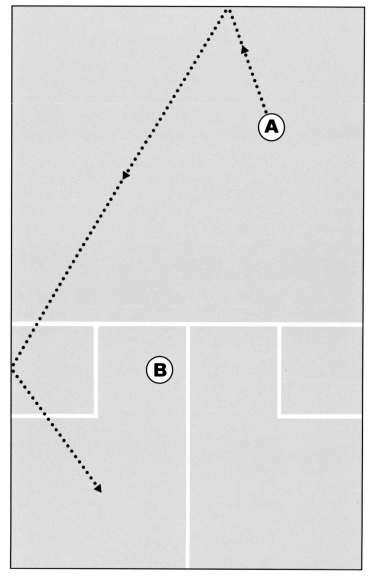

The striker in the front court, committed to a backhand cross-court, has used extra width to beat the threatened volley of his opponent

Use extra width to beat the volley

In order to beat attempted volleys, angle cross-courts and straight drives into the side. Ideally, you will get the ball into the side, just before your opponent wishes to volley. Remember to use extra width when an opponent is standing right up on the 'T' or short line.

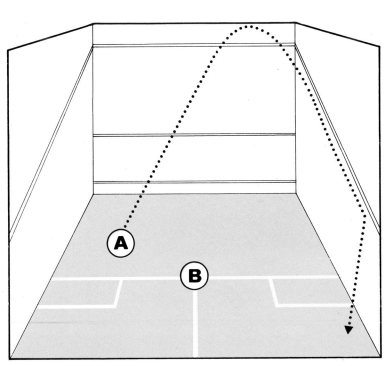

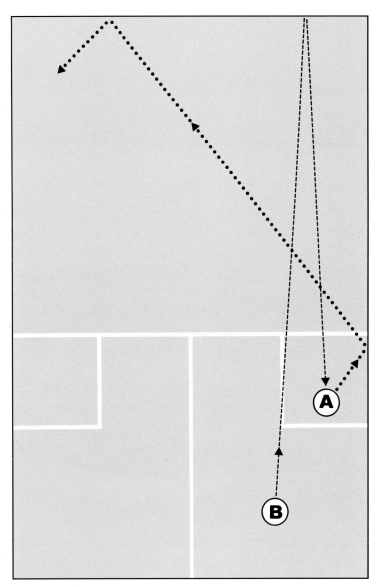

Lob to create time

The lob is the most underrated and under-used shot in squash. It gives you time to recover the 'T' when under pressure, especially when your opponent is right up in position. Do not be tempted to go short. Lob if an opponent is weak on the volley; often a player will be weaker on one side than on the other.

Boast the short ball

Boast the short ball when your opponent is behind: he is out of position and you can move him over a distance to the front. Do not boast when your opponent is in position on the 'T'. Boasting is an excellent move in squash, but if it is overdone or played at the wrong time, it can result in loose play and easy returns for your opponent.

The moves

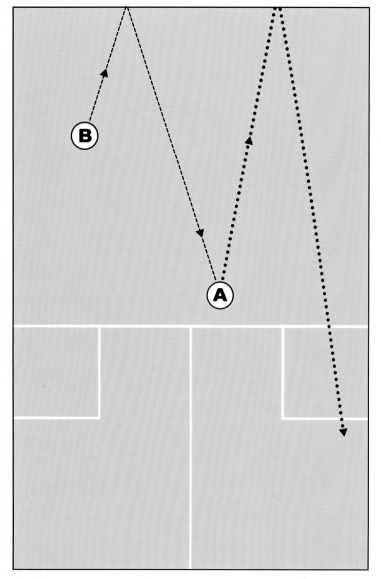

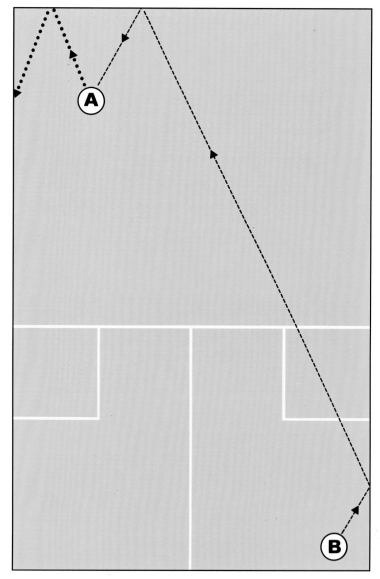

Follow up
Follow up your moves by looking for and anticipating your opponent's next shot. Follow up your attacking boast, and other short shots, by moving up the court and looking for a ball to intercept and volley away to die in the back.

Drop off the boast
Endeavour to force your opponent to boast out of the back, so that you can straight drop. This will move your opponent over the diagonal – the furthest you can make him run.

The striker in the front court has seized on his opponent's weak ball to play a straight forehand drop shot

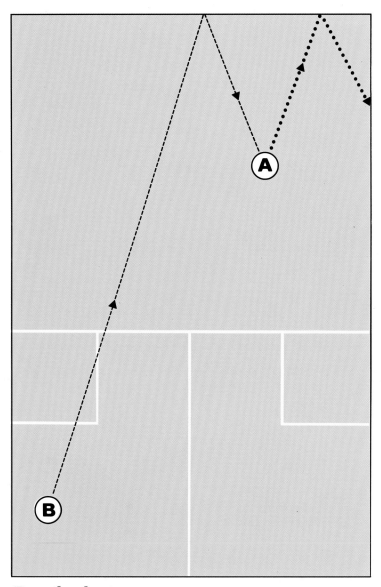

Drop the short cross-court

Dominate the 'T' and keep your opponent back until you get an opportunity to send him short. A standard opportunity is a straight drop off a short cross-court from the back. Again this moves your opponent over the diagonal. It follows the basic positional rule: hit the ball as far away from your opponent as possible.

The moves

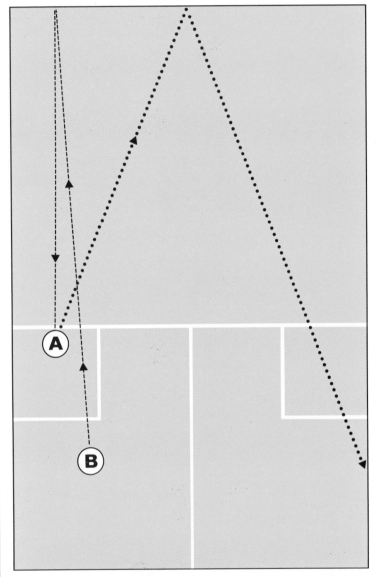

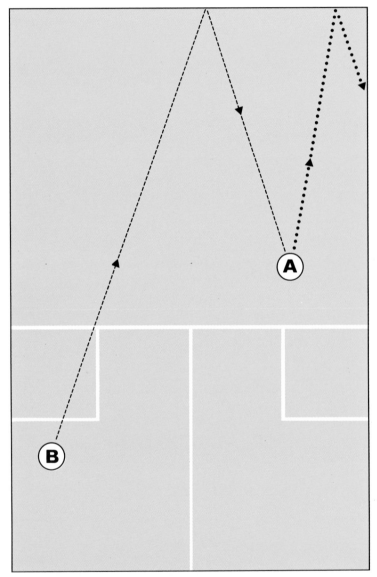

Volley away from an opponent
Look for and take opportunities to volley away from an opponent. Do not take the risk of going short unless the ball is just right. When you have the 'T', you can pull the ball a little shorter to a dying length as you do not need the time to recover. Volley away from your opponent where possible.

Volley drop the loose cross-court
Pin your opponent back and seek out ill-considered and loose cross-courts to volley drop straight.

The player in the back court has played a high loose cross-court. The striker in position on the 'T' seizes this attacking opportunity to play a forehand volley drop. This forces his opponent to move on the diagonal from the back court and pressurizes him into a difficult recovery in the front corner

The moves

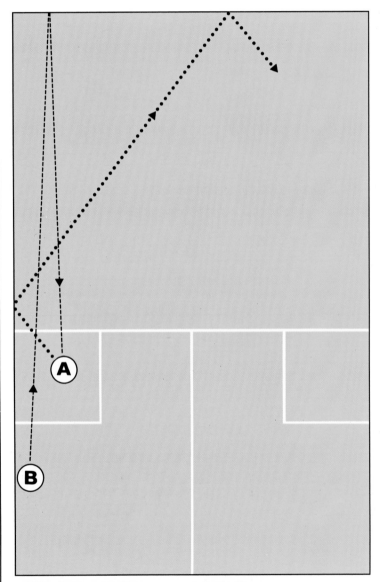

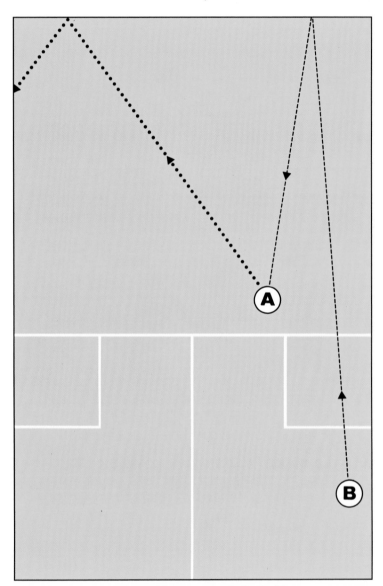

Volley boast the loose straight ball

Again, this will move your opponent over the diagonal. If he has played from the back, you will have an excellent opportunity of catching him out of position.

Cross-court drop the loose straight ball

The cross-court drop is a main source of winners. Aim for the nick. Keep your opponent trapped behind you and play the ball away from him.

Ross Norman responds in mid-court to a cross-court drive from Jansher Khan designed to draw him from the 'T' (top left). As Jansher shows (top right), the 'T' is the power position from which to reach any stretching shot

Lisa Opie occupies the 'T' while sending Lucy Soutter scrambling into the top right corner (bottom left). Martine Le Moignan performs the reverse skill upon Heather Wallace in the top left corner (bottom right)

Match report RELENTLESS DETERMINATION

Event: UAP World Open
Championship Final
Venue: Palais des Sports, Toulouse,
France
Date: 11 November, 1986
Scoreline: Ross Norman (New
Zealand) bt Jahangir Khan (Pakistan)
9–5 9–7 7–9 9–1

The World Open Final in Toulouse was the resounding conclusion of the most determined pursuit in the history of squash, perhaps in the history of sport.

One bright summer day in June 1983 Ross Norman tried his hand at parachuting with devastating results. He fell on the edge of a concrete runway on his first actual jump, turning the top of his left leg in one direction and the bottom in the opposite direction. The action was similar to tearing a turkey drumstick apart at the Christmas table. Technically, he detached the posterior cruciate ligament and tore the medial ligament.

Those who visited him later in the orthopaedic wards of London Hospital gave little hope for a competitive return by the pale and wasted figure they found suspended from the ceiling by wires attached to a steel bar drilled through his left shin. He was twenty-four and ranked eighth in the world. It seemed the limit of his sporting possibilities.

But Ross Norman is a peculiarly tough character. He fought his way back to fitness, worked long and lonely hours re-strengthening the injured leg and driving the rest of his body to new levels of stamina and fitness.

During those long months of pain and work he formed the ambition of beating the mighty Jahangir Khan. He was back in action by the end of 1983 and by early 1984 he was strong enough to reach the semi-finals of the French Open and then the quarter-finals of the British Open. 'I might have done better had it not been Jahangir himself I met at those stages.' Then came another summer of work.

Ross Norman, new World Champion and the man who ended the 5½-year undefeated reign of Jahangir, phones home to New Zealand with the news

No adventures this time, but the gradual firming of the realization that he was becoming stronger and fitter than ever before in his life. 'I found I could eat up training and still come back for more.'

In the 1984–86 seasons Norman took on every commitment available to him. He entered every major tournament in the world. By October 1985 he was established as the world number two, winning everything ignored by the Pakistani maestro and finishing as runner-up whenever Jahangir Khan decided to play. The international circuit became a two-horse race.

They played nine major finals in the 1984–85 season, with Jahangir Khan winning eight times in straight games and the ninth, the World Open Final in Cairo, for the loss of just one game. Between July 1985 and October

1986 Norman lost to no man except Jahangir Khan. The rest of the professionals on the world circuit began to talk of Norman as the 'Iron Man'.

But they viewed his ambition with scepticism. Jahangir Khan's record was even more extraordinary. Every other challenger had been left in the dust. By the time the two met again in the next World Open Final a year later in Toulouse, Norman had lost four more finals without gaining another game and Jahangir Khan was looking back on five years, seven months and a day without a single defeat.

The twenty-four-year-old supreme champion had played more than 500 matches, achieved over 100 tournament victories, since last losing to Australia's Geoff Hunt in the British Open Final of 1981. Norman ended it all, just as he always said he could: 'Some day, somewhere, Jahangir will be off his game and I will be right on, and I will get him.'

He had taken thirty defeats from Jahangir Khan in his career to that point. He chased him doggedly around the world for two seasons, losing on glass courts, plastic courts, and plain old-fashioned plaster courts.

The last step of the great pursuit took an hour and 50 minutes. Norman won 9–5 9–7 7–9 9–1, playing strongly and calmly in strange conditions, against a defending champion off his game. Just as he said he could. It was the end of an era. 'It was an amazing feeling. At last I could let go and shout for joy. I had done it the hard way, worn him off the court, the greatest player this game has seen.'

Jahangir Khan arrived short on match practice and still carrying a

Thirty defeats in his career, but this was the opportunity Ross Norman had pursued doggedly. Every shot counted. Nothing was allowed to stand in his way

slight knee injury. He was for once severely tested in the semi-finals by Australia's Chris Dittmar. And he was unable to adjust to the decidedly odd bounce of the Merco Globall which, painted with reflective stripes for television, skidded and leapt unpredictably on both floor and walls. Norman's concentration was such that he seemed almost unaware of such problems. He took the first game in 28 minutes, commanding play from the back court and allowing Jahangir Khan no time or room in which to set himself for his usual long and short tactics.

The Pakistani hung on in the second game, rarely looking comfortable or balanced, but refusing to give up on a single rally. It took Norman 42 minutes to put that in the bag. Already records were changing. The last man to take two games from Jahangir Khan was Hiddy Jahan, back in the Welsh Masters Final of 1982. In the third game Jahangir Khan moved up court for the early volleys that were his only answer to the skidding ball. Norman slipped behind 2–5, pulled back to 7–7, but eventually lost it in 24 minutes. 'I kept thinking that Jahangir plays his best squash when he is behind. I went on for the fourth telling myself not to panic.'

His fears were groundless. Jahangir Khan was almost spent. Norman won the fourth game in nine minutes but even at 8–1 he was counselling himself: 'You got here playing sensible squash. All you have to do is keep

Courage, determination and the realization that the moment was at hand for victory show clearly in every fibre of Ross Norman's being

playing sensible squash to take out the leader of the pack.'

Jahangir Khan had blown his best effort clinching the third game by taking up the pace from 7–7. When Norman began to fire in long drop shots in the fourth, he just had no heart to chase them. Nobody had seen Jahangir Khan played to a standstill before.

The man surgeons gave only a 50:50 chance of walking properly after his 1983 parachuting accident had won the longest race in squash history. Ross Norman, the Iron Man from New Zealand, was Champion of The World and, perhaps more importantly, the man who ended the total supremacy of Jahangir Khan.

Chapter 6 SQUASH INJURIES

Every sport carries a risk of injury, and squash is no exception. Sports injuries fall into two basic categories: trauma and overuse. Squash players may encounter either type, but overuse injuries are the more common. Specialist treatment is usually needed, but squash players should know how to *cope with emergencies, and how to avoid the preventable injuries. This chapter describes why squash carries such risks, how to minimize them, what some of the common squash injuries are, what immediate action should be taken when they happen, and what treatment is likely to be given.*

Trauma and overuse

A traumatic injury is usually a sudden accident, from which you have immediate symptoms of damage, such as pain, swelling, bleeding or bruising. Examples include being hit by your opponent's racket or the ball; slipping and turning your ankle; or lunging for the ball and tearing your Achilles tendon.

An overuse injury comes on gradually, usually starting with a niggling pain or ache, which then develops into more severe pain if you carry on playing. Typical examples include 'tennis elbow'; Achilles peritendinitis; kneecap pain; or cramp-like muscle strains.

Every squash player should learn basic first aid, in order to be able to cope quickly and efficiently in an emergency. Accidents cannot always be avoided, so everyone involved in

Susan Devoy relies on her strength, the result of long and carefully-programmed weight-training

squash should know how to give effective treatment when an accident happens. The best way to learn first aid is to join one of the classes run by organizations like the St John Ambulance Brigade or the Red Cross.

Risk factors and some antidotes
Squash is a game played in bursts of activity of high intensity, alleviated by short rest phases. It requires physical fitness: it is well established that you need to get fit to play squash, rather than play squash to get fit.

Firstly, your heart and lungs must be working well. Fortunately, it is rare for a squash player to collapse and die on the squash court, but it does happen. In some cases, the player has been known to have had a heart problem. In others, viral infection has often been established as the cause of the collapse. If you have any kind of infection that gives you a fever (raised temperature), or needs antibiotic treatment, you should probably not be playing squash or doing any physical exercise, and you must be prepared to be guided by your doctor as to when you should re-start.

One simple guide to your state of health is to check your pulse count regularly in the morning, when you first wake up. If you are feeling under the weather, and your pulse count is up by ten beats or more, you should

Stretching exercises

Hold one leg behind you, pulling heel towards buttocks until your thigh is stretched. Count to 10, release and repeat on other leg

Leaning against a wall, bend front knee until rear leg calf muscle stretches. Count to 10, release slowly and repeat on other leg

Leaning against a wall and keeping heels flat on the floor, bend the knees to feel stretch in the back of the legs. Count to 10, relax and repeat

probably rest from exercise until it is normal and you feel better. This guide is especially useful when you are recovering from debilitating illnesses like flu or glandular fever.

The second aspect of fitness relates to your body mechanics. Squash places special demands on your muscles, bones and joints. You must have good speed, stamina, strength, and flexibility. Body-conditioning training should contain the necessary elements to improve these factors. A good training programme should include skill practice; stamina work such as shuttle runs, ghosting, skipping or cycling; speed training, usually working on flat-out sprints; strength work, usually weight-training; and flexibility work based on passive stretching and active mobility exercises.

The modern competitive player *has* to do at least some physical fitness training to succeed. Even if you play purely for fun, you should be aware of the importance of fitness. If you are not prepared to work out in a gym, you could try doing other types of sport to improve your fitness.

Movement patterns

The movements involved in squash are specific, and, in some ways, limited. The game involves a lot of crouching and bending, using the legs, hips, and lower back. The shoulder, elbow and wrist of the racket arm are stressed through particular arcs of movement.

Preparing the body for the stresses of each game of squash is important for the player. A thorough warm-up should stretch and mobilize all the major muscles and joints, before moving on to more energetic movements such as sprints or jumps. The warm-up should end with shadow strokes, hitting an imaginary ball with the racket, before going on court. Remember that the ball is cold when you first go on court, but the effort of getting it moving will be less stressful to you if you have thoroughly warmed up beforehand. A warm-down, concentrating on stretching exercises, can help prevent stiffness after the game, and this in turn can prevent muscle strains and overuse injuries.

Players whose only form of physical exercise is squash tend to be stiff in

the knees, hips, back and elbow, and this can influence or even dictate the injuries they suffer. This means that background fitness training should not be geared only to improving your squash-playing ability. It should also include elements to counteract the harmful effects of the game, stretching and strengthening the parts squash weakens or does not reach.

Age and sex

Young players going through their growth phases are vulnerable to injuries due to the stresses squash places on muscles and joints. Overuse injuries are likely to occur if a child learns to play squash using an adult-size racket that is too heavy or cumbersome. Every child should use a junior or cut-down racket until he or she is strong enough to handle a full-size model.

Playing too much (too long or too often) is a common cause of problems in children, especially in teenagers during their growth spurt, affecting their leg, hip and spinal bones. Even for the child with aspirations to stardom, other activities should also be

Trauma and overuse

Stretching exercises

1 Sit with one leg straight out in front of you, the other tucked sideways behind you. From the hips, with straight back and head up, gently lean forward. Count to 10, relax and repeat with other leg

2 With legs out straight and ankles flexed, gently lean forward and hold for a count of 10. Relax and repeat

3 Sit on the floor, soles of feet touching. With head up and back straight, slowly lean forward. Release gradually and repeat

4 Crouch down on one leg with your other leg straight out sideways. Lean gently sideways over extended leg. Count to 10, relax and repeat with other leg

Squash is a close contact sport in which collision is a constant danger. Let rules are designed to prevent accidents

encouraged to avoid injury problems and 'burn-out'.

Women can be particularly vulnerable to squash injuries. The pelvic area, between the hips and lower back, is more likely to be over-strained by the normal shearing stresses in squash at times when the ligament tension is altered by hormonal changes, such as during the pre-menstrual phase, the initial phase of menstruation, pregnancy, and possibly during the menopause. It is also possible that hormonal factors affect the calf muscles, making women players more vulnerable to calf muscle strains or tears, or Achilles tendon rupture (tear) at certain phases of the hormonal cycle.

Older players of both sexes, in the 'vintage' age group, are likely to have a degree of wear-and-tear arthritis in their joints. If arthritic joint pain is aggravated by playing squash, the player should cut down the amount of play, or stop altogether, according to medical advice. In many cases, arthritic joints may be kept strong and mobile by continuing to play, but it is important not to play through pain.

Close contact sport

Opponents on a squash court are in close proximity, moving around each other to have sight of the ball or to reach it. There is a constant danger of collision with each other, each other's racket, or the ball. The 'let' and 'point' rules of the game are designed to prevent accidents. Every player has to be aware of safety, and should understand the rules applying to potentially dangerous situations. In competitions, the referee (or the marker in the absence of a referee) is responsible for safety, and may have to call time if the players play on in dangerous situations.

Technique is an important factor in safety, because the players are so close together. The beginner with a wide, uncontrolled swing is a menace to any opponent. This is a particular problem in tennis players who switch to squash without adjusting their stroke production properly. Beginners can also create danger by turning to watch the opponent behind them instead of watching the front wall and just glancing back; by turning on the ball and therefore striking it too close to the opponent; and by being unable to stop short when making a stroke likely to hit the opponent. The beginner usually needs professional coaching to correct these faults. The more experienced player sometimes creates danger almost deliberately by crowding or baulking the opponent, giving the opponent, marker or referee the difficult job of imposing discipline through the rules.

Playing conditions

Although there are technical regulations dictating how a squash court is constructed, squash courts vary, especially since it has become possible to use glass and Perspex to create transparent walls. Most courts have sprung floors, but some are more rigid than others. Courts built with outside walls and no heating system may be very cold, whereas some are heated to a high temperature, or warmed by being within a larger heated building.

Players have to adjust to different playing conditions, and should be aware of them. For instance, you may need more layers of clothing in the correct colour if you are playing on a very cold court. Before playing a hard

Trauma and overuse

Stuart Davenport recognizes the advantages of sweat-bands above the eyes and on the racket wrist

game on a hot court, you should make sure you have had plenty of water to drink at regular intervals, and you may even need to take sips of water after the knock-up and between games. Putting on a warm tracksuit after playing and before showering is obviously vital in a cold environment, but it is also important in warmer temperatures, to prevent chills.

Court owners and managers have the responsibility of keeping courts safe, but players too should be aware of basic safety factors. A squash court floor should be swept clean, but never polished. Water on the court, whether caused by leaks, condensation, or players' sweat, can make it too dangerous for play. Splinters or uneven boards can catch players' feet and cause falls. Lighting has to be adequate, without any strong contrasts of light and shade. Good visibility is helped by clean walls and ceilings.

The racket
Choosing the right racket can be complicated, especially for the beginner. Wooden rackets may be better for beginners, being cheaper and possibly tougher than those models made in modern alternative materials like graphite and boron. Finding a suitable racket may be a matter of trial and error.

Weight is important: a very light racket may be too 'whippy' for your style of play, whereas a racket that is too heavy inevitably stresses your arm unnecessarily. The balance of a racket is probably even more important. Most players need a racket that is relatively light in the head, as a head-heavy racket can place a dragging

effect on the forearm muscles. Checking a racket's balance is a simple matter of resting the shaft on a pivot so that it lies horizontally. Head size and shape have been the subjects of manufacturers' experiments recently: choosing a larger or squarer-headed racket is simply a matter of personal preference.

The racket grip should be wide and long enough to allow the hand and fingers to spread comfortably around it. If the grip is too wide, the hand may be over-stretched, placing stress on the forearm muscles. A short grip can force you to hold the racket too low on the handle, preventing the proper spread of the fingers, and altering the balance of the racket. Players choose towelling or leather grips according to personal preference: it is important to ensure that the grip is not slippery, and to replace a worn grip immediately.

You have to allow yourself time to adjust gradually, if you make any change in your racket, especially if it is a radical change. Many players find that switching from wood to graphite, boron or composite rackets improves their play, although some good players still prefer wood. Although a new racket may flatter you into thinking it is helping your game, you must be aware that it will also alter the way you produce your strokes. Playing too much, without gradual adjustment, is the most common cause of injuries related to racket change. You should always try out a new racket by using it for short periods, preferably playing less than normal, until you are sure it suits you, and that your game has adjusted to it.

Clothing
The rules concerning clothing on the squash court have been made mainly for safety's sake. For instance, black or dark clothing was not allowed, because it could make it difficult to see the black ball. Now that players use lighter-coloured balls, darker clothing is becoming permissible. For any level of competition, all-white clothing used to be the unbending rule, but now other colours are increasingly accepted.

Players have to use common sense as well. Your clothing should not be tight or loose enough to impede your shot production, or your movement around the court. It should be easy to keep clean, and washed frequently to avoid harmful bacteria and fungi. The materials should 'breathe' easily, so that sweat is transmitted away from your body.

Protective eye-guards have been recommended, to prevent eye injuries, although few players use them, except in countries where they are obligatory. If you wear spectacles to play, you must make sure they are unbreakable. A sweat-band round the forehead can help prevent misting, although it is usually necessary to keep a dry cloth handy to clean the glasses.

Shoes

Squash shoes vary in design and quality. When you choose a pair, you should look for a good fit, allowing some space for your feet and toes to spread out as your feet get hot under the pressure of play. The width of the shoe upper should be matched by a broad enough sole: many cheaper shoes have an overhang because the sole is too narrow for the upper.

Squash shoe materials should 'breathe', so that they do not create extra heat. Canvas used to be the most popular material, but synthetic materials are more common nowadays. The better shoes are lightweight but strong, without too many trimmings or seams to create undue pressure.

You need grip in the sole of a squash shoe, to allow you to pivot and change direction safely. Any shoe that is slippery under the sole or along its edge is likely to make you

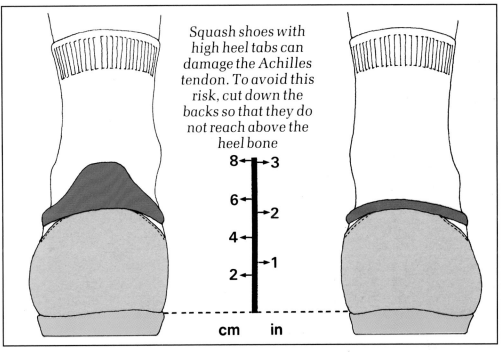

Squash shoes with high heel tabs can damage the Achilles tendon. To avoid this risk, cut down the backs so that they do not reach above the heel bone

slide dangerously. The squash shoe needs quite a thin sole, so that you can feel your foot movements distinctly. A thick sole can prevent you from making quick changes of direction safely. If you need extra cushioning, use a polymer or cellular material insole, or shock-absorbing heel pads.

The heel counter at the back of the shoe should be firm enough to hold the shoe on safely, but it should not be hard or cause friction. The back of the shoe should not reach above the level of the ankle joint: unfortunately, most modern sports shoes have followed a fashion for high backs which can contribute to, or even cause, Achilles tendon problems. To be safe, measure your heel bone, and then the back of your shoe above the sole. Any heel tab or dipped back should be cut down to the height of the heel bone.

Squash shoes should not be kept in a bag after play, but should be allowed to dry out, to avoid fungi and bacteria forming. They should be used only for squash: partly to avoid the danger of getting dirt on the soles, which might form a hazard on court, and partly because a squash shoe is not strong enough to give proper support under continual stress, as in walking or running.

You should check your squash shoes regularly. If the insoles wear down in the heel or forefoot, change them immediately, as they are essential protectors against blisters and shock waves. Never use a torn insole. It is usually simple to slip out the old insole and slide in the replacement. Once the shoe's soles start to wear smooth, or the upper shows tears, it is time to buy new shoes.

First aid and self-help measures

Resuscitation is a technique that should be learned by everyone involved in sport. If a player collapses on court, and the heart and lungs stop working, it is only a matter of seconds before brain cells start to die off because they are deprived of oxygen. It is therefore essential to be able to act quickly in applying mouth-to-mouth or mouth-to-nose resuscitation to restore the victim's oxygen supply. A valved airway can make this process easier and more hygienic, so it is worth learning how to use one, and including it in your basic first-aid kit. A player who has collapsed needs urgent hospital treatment, even after an apparently quick recovery, so you must know where the telephone is, or how to notify attendant staff immediately of the emergency.

Cuts can be caused by blows from a racket. It is usually best to wash a cut under running water, rather than cleansing it with proprietary products. Slit cuts, which tend to happen especially round the eye socket, should be drawn together and held with 'butterfly plasters' or 'steristrips' – thin strips of sticking plaster that anchor the sides of the cut together in the same way as stitches. Deep slit cuts may need stitching, so the victim should go to a hospital. Sticking plasters should be carried in the first-aid kit for bigger cuts or burst blisters. For wounds covering larger areas, or very deep cuts, you should carry sterile dressings in various sizes, to keep the wound protected until the player reaches a doctor or hospital.

Muscle strains or tears and joint sprains are best treated by cold compresses or ice wrapped in a damp flannel, to limit pain and swelling. Compression is an important factor in these injuries, so it is worth keeping lengths of tubular bandage in various widths in your first-aid kit. A crepe bandage on its own does not provide much support, unless it is used over cotton wool wadding. Elevation of the injured part helps to keep swelling under control: this means supporting the injured area upwards in relation to gravity, for instance by holding the hand up in a sling, or lying with the foot supported on cushions for leg injuries. The first-aid treatments of ice, compression and elevation (ICE) may need to be continued for several days after an injury occurs, to control swelling and pain.

Self-help in injury treatment cannot take the place of specialist diagnosis and care. While you should know what to do immediately when an injury happens, the next stage is to refer to your doctor for a diagnosis, any investigations needed, and perhaps referral to an appropriate practitioner, such as an orthopaedic surgeon or chartered physiotherapist.

It is never advisable to play on when you have suffered a painful injury. Playing through pain can only make matters worse, or lead to secondary injuries. You must be prepared to rest from squash until the injury heals. If you try to play too soon, you may suffer the same injury again, or create a muscle imbalance that leads you into a sequence of further injuries. In many cases, you should be doing remedial exercises to help the injury to mend, and you may be able to do alternative training to maintain your fitness. Your rehabilitation prog-

Safety margins in squash are narrow. Top professionals can work this close. Not many others can

ramme will lead gradually to a return to normal training and squash playing. It is always worth trying to work out what might have caused the injury, if it is possible that there is some correctible factor such as overplaying, a change of technique, or a change to a less suitable racket or inappropriate shoes. Understanding the cause of the injury is important in preventing a recurrence of it.

Common squash injuries

Blisters are caused by friction. Under the ball of the foot, they may be caused by a hard game on a hot court, worn or thin insoles, the wrong socks, or shoes with too much grip in the sole. When blisters happen over the top or sides of the foot, it means your shoes are probably too narrow or the wrong shape. It is worth checking your shoes and socks to prevent recurring blisters.

The blister itself should be kept clean with frequent washing with soap and water, and it should be thoroughly dried after washing. It is best not to burst it, if possible. If it is very large and full of fluid, you can pierce it with a sterilized needle, and then cover it with a sterile dressing. You should avoid playing again until it has healed. Foot-care treatment from a chiropodist or podiatrist can help heal and prevent blisters. Any blister that becomes infected should be treated by your doctor.

Stress fractures can happen in any of the foot bones. This is an overuse injury, in which a small crack appears in a bone, due to repetitive stress, for

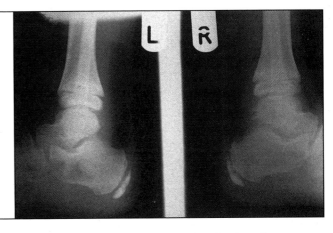

The ankle of this twelve-year-old player has been painfully jarred. Note how the separating growth-line compares to the right heel

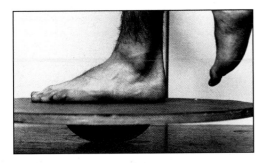

The wobble board re-trains ankle co-ordination after a traumatic injury

instance if you have done a lot of court sprints in one direction, or skipping, especially on a hard surface. Stress fractures only show on an X-ray when they are healing, so if your doctor suspects a stress fracture because the bone is tender when pressed, he will advise you to rest from any painful activities until the bone stops being painful. You will be able to continue any sport or exercise that does not cause pain: this may even include squash, as the varied movements in the game may not stress the particular site of the fracture. Sometimes it is difficult to distinguish between ligament strains and this type of bone fracture, in which case it is best to play safe and avoid any painful activities for as long as it takes (usually 3–5 weeks) for the pain to subside.

Heel bruise is a particular problem in squash, due to repetitive jarring. Young players aged between ten and fourteen are particularly vulnerable to this overuse injury, because the heel bone is growing during this period. If the bone itself is damaged, rest from squash is essential until it has healed. In the adult, this may take

two to three months, but in the growing child it can take six months or more. If the problem is deep bruising in the soft pad under the heel, you may be able to continue squash without pain by putting shock-absorbing pads in your squash shoes. The deep bruise may be helped by daily rubbing with ice, or hot-and-cold dips, and massage with heparinoid cream.

Ankle sprains, or twisted ankles, are traumatic injuries that can happen if you slip on the squash court, especially if you are changing direction quickly and lose your balance. Sometimes worn or smooth-soled shoes contribute to the injury. The ankle should be treated immediately with ice, a bandage from your toes up to your knee, and keeping your weight off it, if it is too painful to walk on. If the sprain is very bad, you should go to a hospital in case it needs X-raying. During the recovery phase, the ankle is best treated by a chartered physiotherapist. The rehabilitation programme will gradually improve the strength and mobility in your ankle. Co-ordination is re-trained through balance exercises, usually

Common squash injuries

using a wobble board. You will not be allowed to play squash again until you can sprint and turn without any pain. You may be taught how to tape your ankle for a degree of support in your first few games.

The Achilles tendon may give pain through a type of overuse injury, usually caused by friction from the backs of your squash shoes. You feel pain when you play, after playing, and particularly first thing in the morning, when it feels very stiff just behind or above the ankle. One or both of the Achilles tendons may be affected. However, the tendon eases out as you get moving, and is painless if you walk, run or jump barefoot. You may need treatment to reduce the pain and any swelling, but the most important factor in recovery and avoiding a recurrence is cutting the backs of your squash shoes so that they no longer rub against the tendon (see page 107).

The Achilles tendon tear or part-tear (total or partial rupture) is a dramatic traumatic injury. The player feels as though the leg has been hit by the opponent, and usually falls over. The injury usually happens when the player is tired, late in the game, and it is more likely to happen if he has been suffering from calf cramps, or, in women, when menstruation is due. To see whether the tendon has broken completely, you gently squeeze the calf muscle: if the foot moves downwards slightly, the tendon is not completely torn, but if the foot remains still, it is a complete rupture. Walking is out of the question, and the player should be taken to hospital as quickly as possible. The surgeon may decide to stitch the tendon together immediately, or the tendon may be protected in a cast, preferably removable so that the injury can be monitored and treated. Recovery is a long process, taking six months or more, and it is vital that the player should be able to sprint and turn confidently before returning to squash.

Calf muscle strains and tears in the back of the leg are less catastrophic. The injury is usually best treated by a chartered physiotherapist, who will aim to recover full mobility and strength in the leg before allowing running, then squash playing. Calf muscle injuries can take six to twelve weeks to mend completely.

Knee cartilages can be injured by sudden twisting strains, or through wear-and-tear degeneration and ageing. A cartilage tear is a traumatic injury, usually causing a lot of swelling round the knee. Ice and a comfortable bandage reaching well above and below the knee must be applied immediately, and the player should see a doctor as quickly as possible, as it may be necessary to drain off fluid. If the cartilage is obviously damaged, the accident or orthopaedic surgeon may decide to operate to remove the torn part immediately. Full recovery from the operation is very quick, between two and six weeks, if the modern method of arthroscopy is used. The physiotherapist will guide the rehabilitation programme so that the knee is fully stable and mobile, before allowing a return to squash.

Overuse injuries to the knee are common in squash players. Teenage players may have problems with the growth points of the knee bones, at the top of the front of the shin or in the kneecap, as squash playing can stress these areas and prevent them from growing together in the normal way. Players of all ages can suffer from strain in the patellar tendon or medial ligament, or pain rising from the kneecap joint. It is vital, once again, not to try to play through the pain, as this can only make the injury worse. The player should be checked by a doctor to decide exactly what is wrong, and to obtain, following this, appropriate treatment. In most cases,

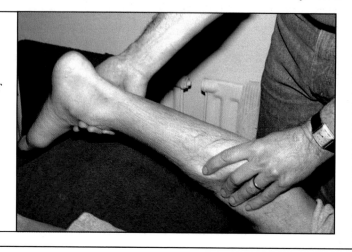

The calf squeeze test determines whether the Achilles tendon has suffered a total or only a partial rupture: the foot will move slightly if the tendon is not completely torn, but if the foot does not move the tendon is totally ruptured

the physiotherapist will advise maintaining stability in the knee through exercises involving twitching the kneecap and pressing the leg straight. The player has to be able to bend and twist the knee without pain before resuming squash.

Thigh muscle strains can happen because of the lunging and quick changes of direction involved in squash. The hamstrings on the back of the thigh and the adductor muscles which reach from the groin down the inner side of the thigh to the knee are very vulnerable in squash players, but the quadriceps group on the front of the thigh can be hurt, too. A sudden tear is a traumatic injury, and the player may feel a 'snap' as the muscle fibres break. This is usually followed by immediate bruising and pain,

which must be treated with ice. The player should avoid stressing the injured muscles in the first few days following the injury, by resting and avoiding walking. Treatment for muscle tears is usually given by a physiotherapist, and the rehabilitation programme aims to restore full flexibility, through passive stretching exercises, and strength in the muscle, before allowing a gradual return to squash.

The thigh muscles may suffer from overuse strains, in which the player feels gradually increasing pain during every game. This type of gradual pain is also sometimes caused by referred symptoms due to nerve pressure in the hip or back, so it is important to seek professional help to establish the diagnosis, preferably

through the general practitioner in the first instance. Treatment can then be directed to the source of pain: if it is an overuse muscle injury, the programme works towards restoring full muscle function; if the pain is referred, the hip or back must be treated, and remedial exercises are aimed at improving function in both the back and the leg.

Pelvic and back injuries

The quick bending and twisting movements of squash stress the hips and back, so injury can occur relatively easily when you are tired, or stiff from previous hard games, or if you simply overreach, or turn too sharply. Women players are especially vulnerable to pelvic and lower back strains just before, or at the beginning of, menstruation. An acute, sudden injury causes immediate severe pain, usually accompanied by muscle spasm, or a type of cramp. In overuse injuries, the pain starts gradually, but can build up to become severe. In either case, ice can be used to ease the pain and spasm, and the player should rest, preferably lying down. Lying flat may be uncomfortable, but lying on your stomach with a pillow under your hips, or lying on your back with your knees bent, may help to ease the discomfort.

Specialist help should be sought as quickly as possible, preferably through the general practitioner.

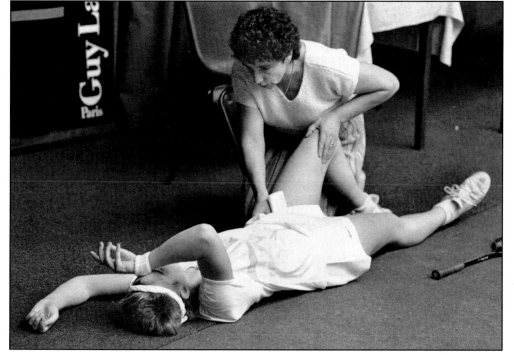

Players of all ages can suffer knee problems. Here Melissa Fryer, one of England's most promising juniors, is receiving instant treatment after leaving the court in severe pain

Common squash injuries

There are many different types of damage that can cause back and pelvic pain, so curing the problem may not be a simple matter. Treatment may be needed from one or more of a number of practitioners, including a rheumatologist (joint specialist), orthopaedic surgeon, physiotherapist, chiropractor or osteopath. The family

Squash puts stress on young joints, and contorting the body can damage the knees which are particularly vulnerable during the growth spurt

Women squash players are very susceptible to back and pelvic injuries, especially prior to or at the beginning of menstruation

doctor is best placed to decide which practitioner is suitable for each case.

As the back is under great stress during squash, you should never try to play when it is painful. You may be allowed to do less stressful fitness activities like swimming, cycling, and some gym work. You will probably be set protective remedial exercises to help stabilize the back, which you will be expected to continue for some time after recovery. Posture is an important factor in any pelvic or back problem, as you can make matters much worse if you sit or stand

badly, placing load or shearing stress on your pelvic or spinal joints.

Useful protective exercises, which may help prevent a recurrence of your back problem once you have recovered, include the bent-knee sit-up; back extension movements lying on your stomach; trunk side-raises lying on either side; and hanging by the hands to relax all the spinal joints.

Shoulder and arm injuries
Shoulder injuries from squash tend to be overuse problems, starting as niggling pains, which gradually get worse. They are usually either tendon or bursa injuries – a bursa is a natural cyst that lies between one tendon and another, or between a tendon and the arm bone below it, to allow friction-free movement.

You must rest from squash while the shoulder is painful. With any arm injury, you should try to analyse whether your playing technique or your racket have had a part in causing the problem. Most shoulder injuries need treatment, possibly from a doctor or a physiotherapist. Recovery depends on regaining strength in all the shoulder muscles, coupled with painless flexibility.

Tennis elbow is a common overuse problem in all racket sports, including squash. It is complex, because many different types of tissue damage may be called 'tennis elbow', and this is one of the reasons why it may be difficult to treat effectively. Therefore it is important to stop playing and see your doctor as quickly as possible to start the necessary analysis of the problem. The simplest version of tennis elbow is tendon strain on the outer side of the joint. This causes pain when you grip objects like the racket handle. At first it may only cause pain when you play, but if it is allowed to develop, you may find the elbow hurts when you lift a kettle or teacup, when you carry a bag, or even when you write.

Tennis elbow can be caused by changes in playing style; poor technique, such as the beginner's 'dropped wrist'; a new racket of a different weight or balance; a change in grip size; or simply by playing more than usual. Your own analysis can help to solve the problem and prevent a recurrence. You can check on grip size influence, for instance, by squeezing a narrow object like a pencil, and then a wide object like your wrist. If one is more painful than the other, it may

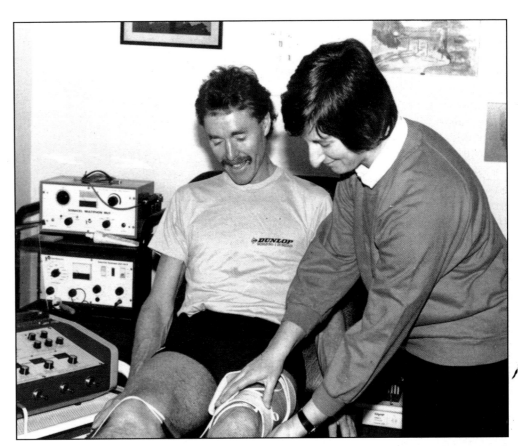

help to adjust your racket grip size, making it narrower, for instance, if the wide-grip action hurts you more.

Treatments for tennis elbow are various, including injection; a range of physiotherapy modalities like ultrasound, interferential therapy, diadynamic currents, faradism, deep massage, and passive stretching for the injured tendon; and, in the last resort, surgery. Sometimes, when all else fails, the problem heals itself after several months. It is important to try to avoid aggravating the problem by continuing activities and movements that hurt the elbow, until the problem is completely cured.

Ross Norman, who wrecked his knee in a parachuting accident, returned to the game, with the help and guidance of Vivian Grisogono, to become World Champion

Chapter 7 DIET

People who exercise regularly often ignore the importance of a correct diet. It is a myth that because you are burning up calories on the court or in the gym, you do not need to worry about what you eat and drink. Your body weight and composition are crucial factors in how you perform on the squash court, but food should provide a lot more than just calories. Similarly, it is not only what you eat, but when you eat that can affect your game. Irregular eating patterns will do nothing to help you achieve better performances; in fact, you could well find yourself losing to opponents you have always beaten in the past. A good diet is above all an on-going affair and not something you should consider only on match days. This chapter offers advice on correcting a poor diet so that you can improve your overall ability and play successful squash.

The essential ingredients

Taking positive steps to improve a poor diet can help your game enormously. Achieving the correct balance is paramount: although we need energy in the form of calories we also need a lot more besides. Cars provide a useful analogy for the way in which we burn up energy: they need fuel, but they also need oil, water, air in the tyres and batteries topped up with distilled water in order to function efficiently. In the same way, we need protein, vitamins, minerals and dietary fibre as well as carbohydrates and fat for fuel.

Protein
Protein is part of the essential structure of all cells. Smaller units, called amino acids, join together to form long chains of protein. Although there are only twenty amino acids, they can combine to make thousands of different proteins, each with its own particular function. Protein-containing foods are digested and

What you eat as well as when you eat can seriously affect your game. Squash players need to establish a well-balanced diet to ensure optimum performance

broken down into amino acids which can then join together to form proteins specific to the human body. Of the twenty amino acids, eight are essential and must be supplied by the diet. The remaining, non-essential amino acids can either be supplied by food, or made in the body.

Any protein not required for body repair and maintenance cannot be stored but must be broken down. The nitrogenous part is excreted in urine and the rest is converted into fat or glucose and stored or used as an immediate source of energy. Protein supplies 4 kilocalories per gram. There is an age-old misconception that sportsmen need more protein than less active people in order to 'build' muscles. Muscle size, however, is determined by the physical demands of training – consuming extra protein as steaks or protein drinks will have little effect. In fact, excessive protein intakes are not only wasteful but can put an unnecessary strain on the body. There is no shortage of protein in the UK diet. Most people eat far more than their bodies need, which can contribute to an unwanted increase in body weight.

We get protein from animal products (e.g. meat, milk, cheese and eggs) and from plants (e.g. cereals, pulses and nuts). People often believe that animal protein is better than plant or vegetable protein. Indeed, they used to be called first and second-class proteins respectively. This view is not really accurate. It is true that animal proteins have amino acid patterns more similar to those in our own bodies but by combining different vegetable proteins a similar picture emerges. In fact, just the regular inclusion of foods such as peas, beans, lentils and nuts will supply quite adequate amounts of essential amino acids.

Carbohydrate and dietary fibre

Carbohydrate is used in the body to supply energy. The term covers both starches and sugars, but all carbohydrates provide the same amount of energy – approximately 4 kilocalories per gram. Dietary fibre is a material found in plants and it tends to be classed with carbohydrates although this is not totally accurate. Strictly speaking, it is not a nutrient, being neither digested nor absorbed by the body. Low-fibre diets have been linked not only with constipation but with disorders of the digestive system, varicose veins, obesity and diabetes. There is general agreement that an increase in fibre intake would be beneficial in helping to prevent these diseases. Modern dietary recommendations require that we also eat more starches but without increasing our sugar consumption.

By grouping carbohydrates according to a traffic-light system, it becomes a relatively simple operation to meet these recommendations. If you switch to foods in the green group you will not only increase your starch intake but also your fibre intake as well. Concentrate less on the amber group and even less on the red group. For sportsmen with a high energy requirement it is not necessary to exclude the red group totally, as long as the major carbohydrate contribution comes from the green group.

A word of caution: simple sugars

Green carbohydrates

- Wholegrain cereals
- Wholemeal flour and bread
- Wholemeal pasta
- Brown rice
- Potatoes and starchy root vegetables
- Pulses: beans, peas, lentils
- Nuts, preferably not salted
- Fruit, fresh, dried or canned in natural juices

Amber carbohydrates

- White flour and bread
- Ordinary pasta
- White rice
- Other breakfast cereals: cornflakes, rice crispies
- Instant potatoes

Red carbohydrates

- Sugar, sweets and chocolate
- Jams, honey, marmalade, golden syrup, treacle
- Breakfast cereals, coated in sugar
- Sugary cakes, biscuits and pastries
- Jellies and instant puddings
- Fruit in syrup
- Sugary drinks: squashes, fizzy drinks

such as glucose and sucrose (ordinary sugar) are absorbed and used quickly, resulting in an increased blood glucose level. The body does not like such sudden rises and so by control mechanisms brings it down. Glucose is removed from the blood and stored, but unfortunately this often results in an over-shoot or rebound action. More glucose is removed than necessary, so you actually end up with a low blood glucose level. Eating sugary foods in the hope of gaining quick energy can, therefore, cause reactive

The essential ingredients

hypoglycaemia or 'highs' and 'lows'. Complex carbohydrates (green group) not only supply more nutrients and fibre than sugars (red group), they also provide a longer-lasting energy supply.

Glycogen is a substance, similar in composition to starch in plants, that is made from glucose by animals – including human beings. It is stored in the liver and muscles and acts as an energy reserve. During exercise these glycogen stores provide the energy you need and, as exercise continues, the stores are used up. It is vital that you replenish them immediately after exercise and certainly before your next bout. It is possible to increase the glycogen stores by eating a high-carbohydrate diet. Studies have shown that muscles carry on working significantly longer after a carbohydrate-rich diet. In other words, the point when fatigue sets in is directly related to the amount of stored glycogen.

Fat
Fat is a very concentrated form of energy. Weight for weight, it provides more than twice as much energy as carbohydrate or protein – 9 kilocalories per gram. Butter, oils, lard and margarine are almost pure fat, but a good percentage of the fat in our diet comes from less obvious sources.

The man who got it wrong. A quick cigarette and a cup of cold coffee accompany the dejection of another defeat. Diet, exercise and smoking habits are within our own control

There is 'hidden' fat in lean meat, egg yolks and peanuts as well as in pastries, cakes and biscuits. The only fat-free foods are fruits, most vegetables, sugar and egg whites.

We need some fat in the diet to provide essential fatty acids, a carrier for fat-soluble vitamins, and to increase the flavour appeal and satiety value of the food. People who eat diets containing a lot of fat, especially the saturated fat in animal foods (meat, cheese, milk and butter) are considered to be at greater risk of suffering heart disease. It must be stated that diet is just one of a multitude of causal factors which include smoking, stress, lack of exercise, sex, age and genetics. However, you can do something about your diet, exercise and smoking habits, but you cannot change your age or sex or your parents if there happens to be a family history of heart trouble. Do not be fooled into thinking that because you exercise, it

does not matter how much fat you eat. At the moment, the average UK diet provides 40 per cent energy as fat, 11 per cent as protein and 45 per cent as carbohydrate (the remainder as alcohol). Not only is the general public being urged to increase the carbohydrate content of the diet to 50 per cent – at the expense of fat – but sportsmen should consider aiming for 55 per cent or more. In short, the extra energy requirement for exercise should come from carbohydrate, not fat.

Vitamins

Vitamins can be divided into fat-soluble vitamins – A, D, E and K – which when eaten in excess to requirements can be stored in the body, and water-soluble vitamins – B complex and C – where excess is simply excreted in the urine. Obviously, you need a regular, daily intake of the water-soluble ones. The table overleaf gives a quick reference to each essential vitamin, its food sources, what it does in the body and how much is needed. Looking at this table, it soon becomes apparent why a varied diet is so important.

The basic diet of a squash player differs from his less active neighbour only in terms of quantity. You will need more energy and nutrients, but these will increase in proportion to each other. If you are choosing the correct foods to meet your energy requirement you should automatically be adjusting your vitamin intake to match. Any marginal deficiency in the basic diet will be reflected in a squash performance below par. If this is the case, the diet as a whole should be improved rather than just resorting

to a vitamin supplement.

Vitamin supplements are singled out most frequently as potential aids to sports performance. There seems to be a belief that they may make the small but so important difference between you and your opponent. The story goes something like this: vitamins are essential for life; vitamins are good for you; therefore, taking extra vitamins must be even better. But can a vitamin supplement actually improve performance if the diet is already perfectly adequate? There is no satisfactory data to confirm this. Any benefits that may have been shown in studies have come from correcting a deficiency, not from taking any 'extra' vitamins. Vitamin C (ascorbic acid) is often singled out for special attention. It is important in tissue repair and certainly a low intake results in slower healing. But, again, there is no conclusive evidence that there is any benefit in supplementing an already satisfactory intake. A bad cold can hinder performance and taking large doses of vitamin

---

Cutting down your fat intake

- Spread butter or margarine thinly
- Trim off fat from meat
- Buy lean cuts of meat and low-fat meat products
- Eat more white fish, but not fried
- Drain off oil from canned fish
- Eat more poultry; remove skin as fat layer is directly underneath
- Grill, do not fry food
- Change to skimmed or semi-skimmed milk
- Use lower fat cheeses: Gouda, Edam, Brie and Camembert
- Avoid cream if possible; use low-fat natural yoghurt instead
- Eat less pastry and chocolate

Vitamin supplements: some guidelines

- Choose vitamin supplements that supply 1–2 times Recommended Daily Amount
- Never megadose, i.e. take many times the Recommended Daily Amount
- Always follow the dosage instructions on the pack
- Take a multivitamin preparation rather than single vitamin supplements
- Buy from a pharmacy where you will get professional advice
- Always view vitamin supplements as 'insurance policies' and nothing more

DIET

The essential ingredients

C (1 gram a day) once you have a cold may lessen symptoms, but regular supplementation will not prevent you catching a cold in the first place.

You may find there are times when you cannot control what you eat or balance your diet. Perhaps you are skipping meals or relying heavily on convenience foods and fast-food takeaways. Your energy intake may be adequate but your vitamins may be down. If this pattern of eating continues and, for whatever reason, cannot be changed, you may want to consider a vitamin supplement.

Minerals
There are a number of minerals and trace elements that are necessary for health. They are needed in relatively small amounts, particularly the trace elements. With two exceptions (which are dealt with later in the chapter) you are unlikely to run into any deficiency problems unless you have a very low food intake or a very bizarre and limited diet. The table opposite lists the main minerals, their food sources, functions and recommended intakes. Functions of minerals fall quite neatly into four groups — bone and tooth formation, blood formation, cell regulation and body management. These functions are all particularly important for sportsmen and you should use the table to check that you are getting an adequate intake of all the minerals.

Energy
Energy is often thought of as something good and necessary, helping you work, rest and play, while calories are bad and fattening and must be counted carefully when trying to lose weight. In fact, they are effectively one and the same. The calorie is a unit for measuring heat, one form of energy, just as a gram is the basic unit for measuring weight. The calorie is a very small unit, so nutritionists use the Calorie or kilocalorie (shortened to kcal) which is a thousand times bigger than the calorie. Sometimes

Vitamin	Food sources	Function	RDA*
Vitamin A	Dairy produce, margarine, liver, green/yellow/orange vegetables, fish liver oils	Essential for proper functioning of eyes, maintenance of healthy skin, hair and nails	a 750μg b 750μg
Vitamin B₁	Wholegrain cereals, meat, pulses, nuts	Production of energy from carbohydrates	a 1.3mg b 1.0mg
Vitamin B₂	Milk, meat, liver, cereal products	Production of energy from carbohydrates	a 1.6mg b 1.3mg
Nicotinamide Niacin, nicotinic acid	Meat, liver, wholegrain cereals	Nerve function, healthy skin and digestion	a 18mg b 15mg
Pantothenic acid	Traces in most foods especially wholegrains, meat, liver	Energy release from fats and carbohydrates	None set in UK
Vitamin B₆ Pyridoxine	Meat, wholegrains, pulses	Essential for brain and nervous system. Needed for blood formation	None set in UK
Vitamin B₁₂ Cyanocobalamin	Meat, fish, dairy produce. Does not occur in plant foods	Needed for blood formation and functioning of nervous system	None set in UK
Vitamin C Ascorbic acid	Fruit and vegetables, citrus fruit and potatoes especially	General maintenance of body. Iron absorption, wound healing	a 30mg b 30mg
Vitamin D Cholecalciferol	Dairy produce, action of sunlight on skin	Maintenance of teeth and bones. Aids absorption of calcium	Supplements unnecessary if sufficient exposure to sunlight
Vitamin E Tocopherol	Vegetable oils, green vegetables, wholegrain cereals, liver	Anti-oxidant effect, protects fatty acids	None set in UK
Vitamin K	Green, leafy vegetables, liver	Clotting of blood	None set in UK
Biotin	Meat, vegetables, offal (liver, kidney), nuts	Processing of fats in the body	None set in UK
Inositol	Oats, yeast, liver, pulses	Energy production from fat	None set in UK

*Reference: Recommended Daily Amounts of Food Energy and Nutrients for Groups of People in the United Kingdom. DHSS, 1979

a Very active men aged 18–64 years old
b Very active women aged 18–54 years old

Mineral	Food sources	Function	RDA† X
Calcium	Dairy products, dark green vegetables, bread, flour (if fortified). Hard water (unboiled)	Structure of bones and teeth. Blood clotting. Muscle and nerve function	a 500mg b 500mg
Chromium*	Brewer's yeast, wholegrain cereals, vegetables	Involved in glucose utilization. Enhances action of insulin	None set in UK
Copper*	Green vegetables, liver, wholegrain cereals, shellfish	Production of many enzymes	None set in UK
Iodine	Seafish, milk, iodized salt, vegetables	Thyroid hormone production	None set in UK
Iron	Offal, meat, eggs, wholegrain cereals	Haemoglobin formation, transport of oxygen	a 10mg b 12mg
Fluorine	Tea, tap water, seafish	Structure of teeth	None set in UK
Magnesium	Most foods, especially green vegetables, cereals, dairy produce, meat	Found in bones and enzymes. Energy metabolism, nerve and muscle function	None set in UK
Manganese*	Wholegrain cereals, nuts, tea, green vegetables	Co-factor for several enzymes (i.e. needed for enzymes to function)	None set in UK
Phosphorus	Most foods. Exceptions: sugar, fats and alcoholic spirits	Bone and tooth structure, metabolism	None set in UK
Potassium	Most foods. Exceptions: sugar, fats, oils and alcoholic spirits	Functioning of all cells, especially nerves	None set in UK
Selenium*	Cereals, meat, nuts	Involved in defence systems of cells	None set in UK
Sodium	Salt, salty foods, meat, fish, cheese and milk	Water balance control, nerve and muscle function	None set in UK
Sulphur	Protein foods: meat, fish, milk, eggs, cereals	Component of some essential amino acids	None set in UK
Zinc	Meat, dairy produce, eggs, fish, wholegrain cereals, pulses	Production of many enzymes	None set in UK

†*Reference:* Recommended Daily Amounts of Food Energy and Nutrients for Groups of People in the United Kingdom. DHSS, 1979

X For the majority of minerals/trace elements, it is believed that they occur in sufficient quantity in a large number of foods. RDAs have, therefore, not been set

a Very active men 18–64 years old
b Very active women 18–54 years old

* *Trace elements*, needed in minute amounts in the diet

you will come across the kilojoule (kj) which is the general unit for measuring all forms of energy. It was agreed internationally that it should be used in preference to the kilocalorie, but there has been a certain reluctance to change. Perhaps the kilocalorie has been around too long, but it is still the unit used most often.

You need energy to keep the body going, e.g. for breathing, digestion, circulating the blood and, in the case of babies and children, growth. You also need energy for all the physical activity you do, not only the exercise on the squash court, but all the daily activities such as walking, climbing stairs, lifting and carrying, even small efforts such as dressing, washing and movements involved at work. The more active your job, the more your energy requirement will increase.

As the food you eat is digested, it is broken down into small units which can be absorbed by the body and used to produce energy or, in the case of protein, to repair body cells. If you eat more carbohydrate and fat than you need for energy or more protein than you need for repair, your body will store the excess as fat. On the other hand, if you do not eat enough food to meet your energy requirements, the body will use the available protein to supply energy at the expense of cell repair. In other words, the body's primary requirement is energy.

The harder and longer you exercise on a regular basis, the greater your energy requirement will be. The extra energy needed by different people can vary between as much as 400 and 2,000 kcals a day (a day when you exercise, that is!). You probably know

The essential ingredients

someone with a similar build to yours who plays as often as you, yet keeps to the same body weight while eating far more than you. That is one reason why it is difficult to predict energy requirements. The best indication that you are matching your own energy requirements is a stable body weight.

Fluid

When you exercise, the chemical energy in the stored glycogen and fat is converted to mechanical energy and a lot of heat is given off as a by-product. As the body maintains its temperature within very narrow limits, this extra heat must be lost from the body. This is done by sweating. As the sweat evaporates from the skin it brings the temperature down. (Sweat that drips off does not contribute to the cooling process.) The amount you sweat depends on the environmental temperature, the humidity and the amount of air movement as well as the actual degree of physical exercise. You must, therefore, be aware of the court conditions before you play so that you can make the necessary arrangements, e.g. available drinks, towels and possibly even a dry shirt.

Sweat does not consist of just plain water but it contains a variety of electrolytes including sodium, potassium, calcium, magnesium and chloride. The actual composition varies between individuals and between the same individual playing on different occasions. Although beneficial in bringing down body temperature, sweating can lead to dehydration which can be more crucial in causing fatigue in a long match than lack of energy. Endurance capacity (length of time you can go on exercising) can be increased if fluids are taken during the period of exercise.

Alcohol

Alcohol is metabolized to produce energy (7 kcals per gram) but unlike carbohydrate and fat it cannot be used directly by muscles during exercise. It is also metabolized slowly and at a constant rate so it is not a good source for rapid energy needs.

Absorption of alcohol is rapid and it is transported by the blood to more or less all parts of the body. The rate of absorption is related to the concentration, neat spirits being absorbed more rapidly than beers. The state of the stomach also affects the rate – absorption is much quicker on an empty stomach. Apart from this, there are two very good reasons why you should avoid alcohol *before* a match. Alcohol is a vasodilator which means that it causes all the small blood vessels to open up and so diverts blood away from vital tissues, such as muscles, to the skin. Secondly, it is a diuretic and, therefore, makes you excrete more urine, causing a drain in body fluid resulting in dehydration. That is why you feel dry-mouthed and thirsty after a heavy drinking session.

Evaporating sweat brings down body temperature, but the sweat that drips from the body can lead to dehydration. The right arrangements for playing conditions, drinks, towels, even dry clothing, are essential for safety and comfort

Balancing your diet

How do you know which foods to eat so that you are getting the right balance of nutrients? No one has the time or inclination to go around with a pocket calculator working out how much protein or fibre they have had. We buy, eat and enjoy *food*, not nutrients, so here is a simple group system that lets you build up a healthy diet without having to worry about individual nutrients. Whenever you can, you should build each meal around the basic four groups. There will, of course, be occasions when you do not choose or prepare your own meal. In which case, if it is difficult to have the right sort of foods at your midday meal, use the evening meal to compensate. Perhaps you missed out on fruit and vegetables, so have an extra helping in the evening. Intakes of nutrients will vary from meal to meal, but the total intake over the day, and certainly averaged out over the week, must meet current accepted standards – and will if you use the 'basic four'.

The lesser groups will be needed by those with particularly high energy requirements or for those times when there are no other foods available. Remember, if you are low on energy either before or after a match, a packet of biscuits or a bar of chocolate is better than having nothing at all. Use these two groups as extras after you have had your quota from the 'basic four' or as emergency rations.

The number of meals most people eat is largely a matter of habit. Many still keep to the traditional pattern of breakfast, lunch and evening meal, while others survive on one or two meals, often eating the main meal late

at night. It has been shown that consuming the same amount of food in one or two large meals leads to an increase in body weight and in the level of certain fatty substances in the blood. We seem to make better use of food eaten according to the adage 'little and often'. Physically active people with high energy needs may not be able to eat enough at one or two sittings and they should adopt the following eating pattern: breakfast, mid-morning snack, lunch, mid-afternoon

and pre-match snacks and, finally, a not-too-late supper to replenish glycogen stores. Less regular squash players will only need to adopt such a pattern on playing days, resorting to a three-meal-a-day pattern on less active days.

Body weight and composition

If you look at the top squash players, there is one thing you will notice immediately – not one of them is overweight or carrying a spare ounce of fat. However, it is not so much the weight that is important as the composition of the body. The table below shows the normal composition of a man weighing 65kg/143lb. Women, on average, have twice as much body fat physiologically as men. Of that 9kg/19.8lb fat only about 1kg/2.2lb is

essential, the rest acts as a store which can be drawn on when needed. In people who are overweight, this store can amount to considerably more and make up a large part of the total body weight. As 1kg/2.2lb body fat supplies 7,700 kilocalories (far more than you would need for a hard game of squash) you may be carrying around considerably more fat than you could ever need. Extra body fat means that your body has to work that much harder, which can put a large strain on

---

Basic food groups

1 **Cereal foods and starchy vegetables**
Bread, flour, oats, rice, corn, breakfast cereals, pasta, potatoes
Provides: energy, fibre, protein, vitamins, minerals. Little fat

2 **Meat and alternatives** Meat, poultry, fish, pulses (beans, peas, lentils), eggs and nuts
Provides: protein, vitamins, minerals, energy. Fibre from pulses. Fat from meat and meat products

3 **Fruit and vegetables** Fresh, raw and cooked. Especially dark green/yellow vegetables and citrus fruits (oranges, grapefruits, etc.)
Provides: vitamins C, A, folic acid, calcium and iron. Little fat

4 **Milk and milk products** Milk, cheese, yoghurts
Provides: protein, some vitamins, energy, fat, calcium and phosphorus

Lesser food groups

1 **Sugar, sugary foods and drinks**
Sugar, sweets, chocolate, honey, jams and marmalades, sweet biscuits, cakes, jellies, sugary drinks
Provides: energy

2 **Fats and oils** Butter, margarine, vegetable oils, lard, suet, salad cream
Provides: energy, fat-soluble vitamins, essential fatty acids

---

Normal body composition
Man weighing 65kg/143lb

Protein	11kg/24.2lb	17.0%
Fat	9kg/19.8lb	13.8%
Carbohydrate	1kg/2.2lb	1.5%
Water	40kg/88lb	61.6%
Minerals	4kg/8.8lb	6.1%

Balancing your diet

your heart and lungs. There are no benefits to be gained from carrying excess weight on the court.

Charts showing desirable weights for height or formulae such as the body mass index can only be used as general guides because they do not take into account actual body composition. As you get fitter through training, your body fat percentage will fall and your muscle or lean body mass percentage will increase, so you achieve a high muscle to fat ratio. Muscle is more dense than fat so takes up less room for an equivalent weight. Although you look and feel slimmer, the bathroom scales may not register much change. Daily body weight fluctuations of 2–3kg/4–7lb (especially for women) can occur, so do not weigh yourself every day and,

---

Calculating your body mass index

Body Mass Index (BMI) is a more reliable guide than ideal or desirable weight charts.

- Wear indoor clothing and no shoes
- Weigh yourself in kg (e.g. 70kg)
- Measure your height in metres (e.g. 1.8m)
- Square your height (e.g. 1.8 x 1.8 = 3.24)
- Divide weight by height squared (e.g. 70 ÷ 3.24 = 21.6)

Normal range:	20–25
Moderately obese:	25–30
Grossly obese:	over 30

Stuart Davenport, at 6ft 6in the tallest man in international squash, is a perfect illustration of the squash player's requirement to reduce body fat to an absolute minimum

when you do, always use the same scales at the same time of day and wearing the same clothes. In the end, you are the best judge of what you should weigh. How do you feel and look, and are your waist-bands getting tighter?

If you need to lose weight, you must do so gradually and not at the expense of your squash performance. Severely restricted diets are not compatible with exercising hard and regularly. If you cut back too drastically on intake, you will not only lose body fat but also lean body mass, which is precisely what you are trying to build up. For long-term successful results you must combine exercise with a change in overall eating habits. While you are losing weight your energy input (from food and drink) must be less than your energy output (requirement for body maintenance and activity). Once you have reached the body weight you desire, the output and input should be balanced.

Key points to losing weight
- Follow the advice about reducing fat intake
- Avoid the amber and red carbohydrates
- Reduce alcohol consumption as much as possible
- Eat and drink less
- Eat and drink more slowly
- Adopt a regular eating pattern

Muscle is denser than fat. The scales may not register your true condition. Liz Irving, one of the slimmest and fastest of the top women internationals, works constantly with weights and actually weighs more than some of her male colleagues

Balancing your diet

Match days

You will want to arrive at a match full of energy and well-hydrated. Try to have something to eat between two and three hours before your match. This is not always easy because in a team match or competition you will not know exactly when you are going on, but try not to eat less than two hours before you play. This is because you will feel most comfortable if your stomach is empty or nearly empty. You need to allow enough time for food to leave the stomach – high-fat or protein foods take between two and four hours and carbohydrate foods between one and two hours, depending on the size of the meal. To ensure you are fully hydrated drink about

Waiting until you feel thirsty is not advisable. Chris Dittmar of Australia replenishes body fluid with plain water at the end of a game

300–450ml/½–¾pt water 10–30 minutes before play. Do not worry, the blood flow to the kidneys is reduced during exercise, so you will not have to leave the court suddenly.

It is important to keep your fluid intake up during play especially if you tend to sweat a lot. Do not wait to feel thirsty but drink up to 150ml/¼pt chilled water at the end of each game. If you prefer other drinks, make sure they are cold and dilute – very sugary and warm/hot drinks take longer to leave the stomach. After a match you must make good any fluid loss and start to replenish the glycogen stores in the liver and muscles. If you repeatedly go into matches with depleted stores you will start to run into problems of fatigue and loss of stamina. This is particularly important if you are taking part in a tournament over a number of days. The ability of muscles to fill up with glycogen is best straight after exercise. If you can manage only a snack, have sandwiches and cereal bars, keeping chocolate and sugar-based foods for emergencies only. Meals should be based around a good helping of pasta, rice or potatoes. Match suppers of spaghetti bolognese, chicken curry or shepherd's pie are nutritionally correct. Fluid replacement after a match or training session can be quite adequately achieved with plain water. The small electrolyte loss in sweat will be made up from a normal diet.

Special needs

Women should pay particular attention to their iron and calcium intakes. Iron is important in the production of haemoglobin, the red pigment in blood which is responsible for carrying oxygen from the lungs to the tissues throughout the body. If there is a shortage of iron in your diet you may experience symptoms of fatigue and breathlessness, especially when you exercise. Iron deficiency anaemia is more common in women than men

---

Getting enough iron

- Iron from meat and offal (liver, kidney) is better absorbed than iron from cereals, vegetables, fruit and nuts
- Absorption of iron from all sources can be improved by eating vitamin C-rich foods at the same time, e.g. citrus fruits and fruit juices
- Select iron-rich foods as often as possible
- If you do take a supplement (perhaps vegetarian women) never take more than the prescribed dose. Too much iron can be harmful

---

because of the extra loss of iron in menstrual blood. It is, therefore, important to ensure an adequate dietary intake otherwise you will find your capacity to exercise will be reduced.

There is concern that low intakes of calcium can lead to the development of osteoporosis in later life. Osteoporosis, or brittle bones, causes painful, stooped posture, loss of height and an increased risk of bone fractures. It is important to get a good intake of calcium throughout adolescence and early adult life as well as in childhood as the bones continue to accumulate calcium until about the age of thirty-

five. From then on you start to lose calcium. This loss is speeded up around the menopause because of the reduction in oestrogen. Although regular, moderate exercise can increase the amount of calcium deposited in the bones, intensive endurance training in some women has led to the opposite. These women have very low fat levels which causes a fall in oestrogen levels. Menstruation stops and physiologically they behave like menopausal women. This accelerated loss makes them more prone to traumatic and stress fractures. Women squash players should include calcium-rich foods each day and not reduce their body fat to such low levels.

Vegetarians Vegetarian food can supply all the nutrients you need, but you must be aware of the foods that provide protein and the vitamins and minerals others get from eating meat. Protein will be provided by milk and milk products and eggs, as well as cereals, pulses and nuts. Iron in a vegetarian diet comes from pulses, wholegrains, dried fruit, nuts, molasses and dark green vegetables. The high vitamin C content of such diets should ensure adequate iron absorption. Vegetarian diets are usually more varied in content and include plenty of vegetables, fruits and pulses compared with 'meat' diets, so again B vitamins should not cause any problems. Vegans who eat no animal foods at all do have to be very careful

Women should pay particular attention to their iron and calcium intakes. A shortage of iron in the diet can lead to fatigue in exercise

about planning their diets to avoid missing out on certain nutrients. More information, leaflets and advice from The Vegetarian Society, Parkdale, Dunham Road, Altrincham, Cheshire WA14 4GQ.

Chapter 8 THE RULES OF THE GAME

Ease of access and constant reference to the rules of the game go hand in hand with improvement and enjoyment. With the kind permission of the International Squash Rackets Federation, the rules of the international singles game of squash rackets are reproduced here in their entirety. In the brief introduction, Rule 12, which deals with interference, is explained simply and logical- *ly to help you gain a better understanding of this potentially controversial aspect of the game. Use this interpretation as a guide to enjoying competitive squash while maintaining courtesy and safety on the court. This chapter also includes a description of doubles squash, an increasingly popular area of the sport, together with the rules where they differ from the singles game.*

An introduction to the rules of the singles game

In squash, as in every sport, there is a certain amount of legal phraseology contained within the rules of the game. However, do not be put off by this. Only seventeen rules directly affect the players (out of twenty all told), and each rule is given a number followed by a sub-title, making it easy to establish your query, and then refer to the particular rule that deals with it.

Every sport seems to have a rule that is the subject of controversy. Cricket has the LBW rule. Soccer and rugby have the offside rule. The squash equivalent is Rule 12, which deals with interference. That interference does take place in squash is not surprising. There is no net separating the players, and, to make matters worse, both players are in very close proximity to each other. It is inevitable, therefore, that at some stage player 'A' is going to get in the way of player 'B'. Rule 12 deals with this fundamental problem.

If you can master Rule 12, the rest are easy! It is one of the more difficult rules to get to grips with and, for this reason, requires some analysis. The following breakdown and interpreta-

tion, using slightly modified terminology, is designed to help you gain a better understanding of this most important aspect of the game.

What part of Rule 12 has the *most* effect on the movement of players as they manoeuvre their way round the court? The answer is contained within this sentence: 'After playing his shot, a player must make every effort to get out of his opponent's way.' This means exactly what it says. Perhaps more emphasis should be placed on this requirement than on any other, since the whole idea of squash is to keep the game as fluid as possible.

This leads to the next question: to what degree has a player to get out of his opponent's way? The answer is that a player *must* adhere to four fundamental requirements:

1 'A player must not obstruct the opponent in the latter's direct movement to the ball.' This means that a player, having played his shot, must consider his opponent's position on the court, and appreciate that he is entitled to *direct access to the ball.* Therefore, the player must exit by a route that allows his opponent this direct access. In practice, this often

means that the exit route is sideways. It also means that sometimes the route chosen by the player who has just played his shot coincides with the incoming route chosen by his opponent. The consequences of the resulting collision are dealt with later.

2 'A player must give his opponent a fair view of the ball.' What is a fair view? Assessing this requirement takes a little time, but common sense will give you a guide. You will quickly realize during a game that your opponent normally allows you to have little trouble sighting the ball so that you can play it. On occasions, however, the ball comes back so close to him that you are unable to get a fair view of it, and you cannot play it.

3 'A player must give his opponent freedom to play the ball.' This requirement applies to *both* players. As far as player 'A', who has just played the ball, is concerned, he must not only make every effort to get out of his opponent's way and give him a fair view of the ball, but he must also get out of the way so as to allow his incoming opponent freedom to play the ball. Freedom means giving an oppo-

Stuart Davenport and Neil Harvey (right) in a 1987 British Open match that became famous for its physical involvement. Ross Norman and Jansher Khan (far right) compete for playing space in mid-court

nent room for a normal backswing and follow-through. Again, common sense is a reliable guide as to how much freedom a player needs.

As far as player 'B', his incoming opponent, is concerned, he must also adhere strictly to this part of the rule. He must not approach too early or too close so that he impedes in any way his opponent's normal stroke.

4 'A player must make every effort to get to and, where possible, play the ball.' This also means exactly what it says! This part of the rule refers to the duty of the incoming striker, who must make every effort to get to the ball. The referee will not grant a let on the grounds of obstruction unless the incoming striker has convinced him that his speed and direction would have allowed him to get to the ball in time to play it.

The second arm of this rule – 'where possible the opponent must play the ball' – suggests that there is a grey area here, and indeed there is. If player 'A' has played his shot, and, in getting out of the way, he *slightly* interferes with player 'B' on his way in to play the ball, player 'B' is required to make every effort to play the ball in spite of the infringement. If, on the other hand, the interference is more than slight, there is a limit to what is expected of player 'B', and, in practice, the greater the interference, the less the rules require him to play his shot. Again, common sense is a fairly reliable guide.

Dealing with infringements

Now to the punishment section! What happens if a player does not adhere to one of the requirements listed above? The answer is fairly straightforward. There are three possible consequences:

1 If interference occurs and a player 'has not made every effort to avoid causing it' then, providing his opponent was in a position to make a good return, the opponent is awarded a stroke. A 'stroke' means that the opponent wins the rally and scores a point if he was the server. If he was not the server, he takes over the service.

2 If interference occurs and a player 'has made every effort to avoid causing it' then, providing his opponent was in a position to make a good return, a let is played. A 'let' means that the score remains as it is, and the rally is played again, with the same player serving.

3 If the incoming striker is prevented by interference 'from making a winning return', even though his opponent has made every effort to avoid causing it, then a stroke is awarded.

An example of the last situation would be where player 'A' plays a drop shot that goes up but is not unplayable. His opponent, player 'B', moves up quickly to play it, with the court at his mercy, but player 'A' is still scrambling desperately to get out of the way. Interference is caused and player 'B' is prevented from playing what would have been a winning shot – probably a good-length drive towards the back of the court. But how do you determine whether it is 'a winning shot'? The answer to this question is easy. You are entitled to presume that player 'B' (in this instance) would have played the very finest shot possible.

Summary

These then are the essential parts of Rule 12. There are other parts to the rule but this introduction has concentrated solely on those that achieve a fair result to each rally, comparative safety, and continuity of play. The continuity aspect is very important, because as more people watch squash and marvel at the skills and excitement generated by world-class players, it is vital that the number of lets is kept to a minimum. If both players adhere to the simple requirements outlined, then this will be achieved to the benefit of all.

Rules of the international singles game of squash rackets

Approved by the ISRF at its A.G.M. in October 1984 to become effective on May 1, 1985

1 The game, how played The game of Squash Rackets is played between two players, each using a standard racket, with a standard ball and in a court constructed to ISRF standard dimensions.

2 The score A match shall consist of the best of 3 or 5 games at the option of the organizers of the competition. Each game is to 9 points, in that the player who scores 9 points wins the game except that, on the score being called 8-all for the first time, the receiver shall choose, before the next service is delivered, to continue that game either to 9 points (known as 'No Set') or to 10 points (known as 'Set Two'), in which latter case the player who scores 2 more points wins the game. The receiver shall in either case clearly indicate his choice to the Marker, Referee and his opponent.

The Marker shall call either 'No Set' or 'Set Two' as applicable before play continues.

3 Points, how scored Points can be scored only by the server. When the server wins a stroke, he scores a point; when the receiver wins a stroke, he becomes the server.

4 The service

4.1 The right to serve first is decided by the spin of a racket. Thereafter the server continues to serve until he loses a stroke, whereupon his opponent becomes the server, and this procedure continues throughout the match. At the commencement of the second and each subsequent game,

Danny Lee spins the racket to decide who serves first in a match with Adrian Jaski

the winner of the previous game serves first.

4.2 At the beginning of each game and each hand, the server has the choice of either box and thereafter shall serve from alternate boxes while remaining the server. However if he serves a fault which the receiver does not attempt to return, or a rally ends in a let, he shall serve again from the same box. If the server does serve from the wrong box, play shall continue and the service shall count as if served from the correct box, except that the receiver may, if he does not attempt to return the service, require that it be served from the correct box.

Note to Markers

If it appears that the server intends to serve from the wrong box, or either

player appears undecided as to which is the correct box, the Marker shall indicate to the server the correct box.

4.3 For a service to be good, there must be no foot-fault and the ball, before being struck, shall be dropped or thrown in the air and shall not hit the walls, floor, ceiling or any objects suspended from the walls or ceiling; it must be served directly on to the front wall between the cut line and the out line, so that on its return, unless volleyed, it reaches the floor within the back quarter of the court opposite to the server's box. Should a player, having dropped or thrown the ball in the air, make no attempt to strike it, it shall be dropped or thrown again for that service. A player with the use of only one arm may utilize his racket to propel the ball into the air before striking it.

4.4 A service is good when it is not a fault (Rule 4.5) or does not result in the server serving his hand out (Rule 4.6). If the server serves one fault, which the receiver does not attempt to return, he shall serve again. The receiver may attempt to return a fault on the first service and, if he does so, that service becomes good, is no longer a fault and the ball continues in play. A second service fault cannot be played by the receiver.

Note to Referees

The Referee shall decide what is an attempt to play the ball.

4.5 A service is a fault:

4.5.1 If at the time of striking the ball the server fails to have part of one foot in contact with the floor within the service box and no part of that foot touching the service box line (called a foot-fault), part of the foot may project over this line provided that it does not touch the line.

4.5.2 If the ball is served on to or below the cut line but above the board.

4.5.3 If the first bounce of the ball, unless volleyed, is on the floor on or outside the short or half-court lines delineating the back quarter of the court opposite to the server's box.

Any combination of types of faults in the one service counts as only one fault.

4.6 The server serves his hand out and loses the stroke:

4.6.1 If he serves two consecutive faults.

4.6.2 If the ball, after being served, touches the walls, floor, ceiling or any object(s) suspended from the walls or ceiling before being served.

4.6.3 If the server makes an attempt but fails to strike the ball.

4.6.4 If, in the opinion of the Referee, the ball is not struck correctly.

4.6.5 If the ball is served on to or below the board, or out, or against any part of the court before the front wall.

4.6.6 If the ball, after being served, before it has bounced more than once on the floor or before it has been struck at by the receiver, touches the server or anything he wears or carries, whether the service was otherwise good or a fault.

4.7 The server shall not serve until the Marker has completed calling the score.

Note to Officials
The Marker must not delay play by the calling of the score. However, if the server serves, or attempts to serve,

A server must wait on the referee's instruction until the marker has called the score to begin a rally

prior to the calling of the score, the Referee shall stop play and require the server to wait until the calling of the score has been completed.

5 The play After a good service has been delivered the players return the ball alternately until one fails to make a good return. The ball otherwise ceases to be in play in accordance with the rules, or on a call by the Marker or Referee.

6 Good return A return is good if the ball, before it has bounced more than once upon the floor, is returned correctly by the striker on to the front wall above the board, without first

touching the floor or any part of the striker's body or clothing, or the opponent's racket, body or clothing, provided the ball is not hit out.

Note to Referees
It shall not be considered a good return if the ball touches the board before or after it hits the front wall, or if the racket is not in the player's hand at the time the ball is struck, or if the ball is carried on the racket.

7 Let A let is an undecided stroke, and the service or rally in respect of which a let is allowed shall not count and the server shall serve again from the same box. A let shall not cancel a previous fault.

8 Strokes, how won
A player wins a stroke:

8.1 Under Rule 4.6, when the player is the receiver.

8.2 If the opponent fails to make a good return of the ball, unless a let is allowed or a stroke is awarded to the opponent.

8.3 If the ball touches his opponent or anything he wears or carries when the opponent is the non-striker, except as is otherwise provided by Rules 6, 9, 10 and 13.1.1.

8.4 If a stroke is awarded to him by the Referee as provided for in the Rules.

9 Hitting an opponent with the ball
If the ball, before reaching the front wall, hits the striker's opponent or his racket, or anything he wears or carries, the ball shall cease to be in play and:

9.1 If the ball would have made a good return and would have struck the front wall without first touching any other wall, the striker shall win

Rules of the international singles game of squash rackets

the stroke except if the ball, after rebounding from the front wall, strikes a side wall and the striker follows the ball round and so turns, or without so turning, allows the ball to pass around his body, in either case taking the ball on the hand opposite to that of the side wall from which the ball rebounded, then a let shall be allowed.

Notes to Referees

a. This includes the case where the striker plays the ball behind his back or between his legs.

b. If the striker, having turned, or allowed the ball to pass around his body, chooses not to continue the rally due to the possibility of striking his opponent and, in the opinion of the Referee, is able to make a good return, then a let shall be allowed.

9.2 If the ball either had struck or would have struck any other wall and would have made a good return, a let shall be allowed unless, in the opinion of the Referee, a winning stroke has been intercepted, in which case the striker shall win the stroke.

Note to Referees

Where the striker has turned or allowed the ball to pass around his body, a let shall be allowed.

9.3 If the ball would not have made a good return, the striker shall lose the stroke.

Playing the ball between the legs or behind the back, as Phil Kenyon is doing here against Bryan Beeson, does not change the ruling about taking the ball on the hand opposite the side wall from which the ball has rebounded

Notes to Officials

When a player has been struck by the ball as described in Rule 9, the Marker shall call 'down'. The Referee shall assess the trajectory of the ball and make all further decisions.

10 Further attempts to hit the ball

If the striker strikes at and misses the ball, he may make further attempts to strike it. If, after being missed, the ball touches his opponent or his racket, or anything he wears or carries, then if, in the Referee's opinion:

10.1 The striker could otherwise have made a good return, a let shall be allowed, or

10.2 The striker could not have made a good return, he loses the stroke.

If any such further attempt is successful resulting in a good return being prevented from reaching the front wall by hitting the striker's opponent, or anything he wears or carries, a let shall be allowed in all circumstances. If any such further attempt would not have made a good return, then the striker shall lose the stroke.

11 Appeals Appeals to the Referee under Rule 11 should be made with the words 'Appeal Please'.

In all cases under Rule 12 where a let or a stroke is desired, an appeal should be made to the Referee with the words 'Let Please'.

Play shall then cease until the Referee has given his decision. If an appeal under Rule 11 is disallowed, the Marker's decision shall stand. If the Referee is uncertain he shall allow a let except where provided for in Note to Referees on Rule 11.2.2. Appeals upheld are dealt with in each specific situation below.

Note to Referees

Players making a pointing gesture during a rally should be advised that such action is not a recognized form of appeal.

11.1 Appeals on service

11.1.1 An appeal may be made against any decision of the Marker except for a call of 'fault' or 'foot-fault' to the first service.

11.1.2 If the Marker fails to call 'fault' or 'foot-fault' to the first service, the receiver may appeal provided he makes no attempt to play the ball. If the appeal is upheld the service shall be a fault.

11.1.3 If the Marker calls 'fault' or 'foot-fault' to the second service, the server may appeal. If the appeal is upheld, a 'let' shall be allowed, with 'one fault' standing.

11.1.4 If the Marker fails to call 'fault' or 'foot-fault' to the second service the receiver may appeal, either immediately or at the end of the rally if he has played the ball. If the appeal is upheld, the receiver shall win the stroke.

11.1.5 If the Marker calls 'out', 'not up' or 'down' to either first or second service the server may appeal. If the appeal is upheld, a let shall be allowed.

11.1.6 If the Marker fails to call 'out', 'not up' or 'down' to either first or second service the receiver may appeal, either immediately or at the end of the rally if he has played the ball. If the appeal is upheld, the receiver shall win the stroke.

Note to Referees

If the Marker has not called 'one fault' prior to the delivery of a second service and that service is a fault the receiver, if not awarded the stroke, may appeal that the service was a second service, either immediately or at the end of the rally if he has played the ball. If the appeal is upheld, the receiver shall win the stroke.

Zarak Jahan makes a particularly poignant appeal to the referee about the marker's call on his service from the backhand court

11.2 Appeals on play, other than service:

11.2.1 An appeal may be made against any decision of the Marker.

11.2.2 If the Marker has called the ball 'out', 'not up' or 'down' following a player's return, the player may appeal. If the appeal is upheld a let shall be allowed, except that if in the opinion of the Referee:

a. the Marker's call has interrupted that player's winning return, he shall award the stroke to the player.

b. the Marker's call has interrupted or prevented a winning return by the opponent, he shall award the stroke to the opponent.

Note to Referees

In the latter case the Referee shall also award a stroke to the opponent if he is unsure whether the Marker's call was correct.

11.2.3 When the Marker has failed to call the ball 'out', 'not up' or 'down' following a player's return, the opponent may appeal either immediately or at the end of the rally if he has played the ball. If the appeal is upheld, the Referee shall award the stroke to the opponent.

Note to Referees

a. No appeal under Rule 11 may be made after the delivery of a service for anything that occurred before that service.

b. Where there is more than one appeal in a rally, the Referee shall consider each appeal in the order in which the situations occurred.

c. If a return is called 'not up' by the Marker and subsequently goes 'down' or 'out', the Referee, on appeal, if he reverses the Marker's call, or is unsure, shall then rule on the subsequent occurrence.

12 Interference

12.1 After playing a ball, a player must make every effort to get out of his opponent's way. That is:

12.1.1 A player must make every effort to give his opponent a fair view of the ball.

12.1.2 A player must make every effort not to obstruct the opponent in the latter's direct movement to the ball. At the same time the opponent must make every effort to get to, and where possible, play the ball.

12.1.3 A player must make every effort to allow his opponent freedom to play the ball.

Rules of the international singles game of squash rackets

Note to Referees
The freedom to play the ball must include a reasonable backswing, strike at the ball and a reasonable follow-through.

12.1.4 A player must make every effort to allow his opponent, as far as the latter's position permits, freedom to return the ball directly to the front wall, or to either side wall to within approximately one metre of the front wall.

If a player fails to fulfil one of the requirements of Rule 12.1 (1 to 4) above, whether or not he has made every effort to do so, then interference will have occurred.

12.2 If any such form of interference has occurred and, in the opinion of the Referee, the player has not made every effort to avoid causing it, the Referee shall on appeal, or on stopping play without waiting for an appeal, award the stroke to his opponent, provided the opponent was in a position to make a good return.

Note to Referees
In the case of Rule 12.1 the appeal must be immediate.

12.3 However, if interference has occurred but in the opinion of the Referee the player has made every effort to avoid causing it, and the opponent could have made a good return, the Referee shall on appeal, or on stopping play without waiting for an appeal, allow a let, except that, if his opponent is prevented from making a winning return by such interference from the player, the Referee shall award the stroke to the opponent.

Notes to Referees
a. A player who plays on despite in-

Rule 12, the greatest debating point in squash. What is interference? What is freedom? Who decides?

terference forfeits the right of appeal concerning that interference.

b. Where a player's opponent creates his own interference, the Referee shall rule that interference has not occurred unless the player has contributed to it.

12.4 When, in the opinion of the Referee, a player refrains from playing the ball which, if played, would clearly have won the rally under the terms of Rule 9.1 or 9.2, he shall be awarded the stroke.

12.5 If either player makes unnecessary physical contact with his opponent, the Referee may stop play, if it

has not already stopped, and award the stroke accordingly.

Notes to Referees
a. The practice of impeding an opponent in his efforts to play the ball by crowding or obscuring his view is highly detrimental to the game. Unnecessary physical contact is also detrimental as well as being dangerous. Referees should have no hesitation in enforcing Rules 12.2 and 12.5.

b. The words 'not to obstruct' in Rule 12.1.2 must be interpreted to include the case of an opponent having to wait for an excessive follow-through of the player's racket.

c. A player's excessive backswing may create interference when his opponent has made every effort to avoid such interference. In this case if the player appeals for a let he shall not be awarded the stroke.

d. When, in the opinion of the Referee, a player's swing is excessive and is considered to be dangerous, the Referee shall apply Rule 17.

13 Let, when allowed
13.1 A let may be allowed:
13.1.1 If, owing to the position of the striker, the opponent is unable to avoid being touched by the ball before the return is made.

Note to Referees
This Rule shall be construed to include the cases where the striker's position is in front of his opponent and makes it difficult for the latter to see the ball, or where the striker shapes as if to play the ball but changes his mind at the last moment, preferring to take the ball off the back wall, and the ball in either case hits his opponent, who is between the

striker and the back wall. This is not, however, to be taken as conflicting in any way with the duties of the Referee under Rule 12.

13.1.2 If the ball in play touches any article lying on the floor:

Note to Referees
Referees must ensure that no articles are placed on the floor by the players.

13.1.3 If the striker refrains from hitting the ball owing to a reasonable fear of injuring his opponent:

Note to Referees
This rule shall be construed to include the case of the striker wishing to play the ball on to the back wall.

13.1.4 As provided for in Rule 12;
13.1.5 If, in the opinion of the Referee, either player is distracted by an occurrence on or off the court;

Note to Referees
This shall include the case of an obvious late call on the first service by the Marker.

13.1.6 If, in the opinion of the Referee, a change in court conditions has affected the result of the rally.

13.2 A let shall be allowed:
13.2.1 If the receiver is not ready, and does not attempt to return the service;
13.2.2 If the ball breaks during play;
13.2.3 If the Referee is asked to decide an appeal and is unable to do so;
13.2.4 If an otherwise good return has been made, but the ball goes out of court on its first bounce;
13.2.5 As provided for in Rules 9, 10, 11, 16.1, 17 and 19.5.

In order for a let to be allowed in any of the Rules 13.1 (2 to 6) and 13.2.5 above, the striker must have

been able to make a good return.

13.3 No let shall be allowed when the player has made an attempt to play the ball except where the Rules definitely provide for a let, namely Rules 9, 10, 11, 13, 16.1, 17 and 19.5.
13.4 Unless an appeal is made by one of the players, no let shall be allowed except where the Rules definitely provide for a let, namely Rules 9, 10, 12, 13, 16.1, 17 and 19.5.

14 The ball
14.1 If a ball breaks during play, it shall be replaced promptly by another ball.

Note to Referees
The Referee shall decide whether or not a ball is broken.

14.2 At any time, when the ball is not in actual play, another ball may be substituted by mutual consent of the players or, on appeal by either player, at the discretion of the Referee.

Note to Referees
Either player or the Referee may examine the ball at any time it is not in actual play, to check its condition.

14.3 If a ball has broken but this has not been established during play, a let for the rally in which the ball broke shall not be allowed once either the receiver has attempted to return the next service or the server has served his hand out with that service.
14.4 Where a player wishes to appeal about a broken ball, the appeal must be made before the next service is returned by the receiver or, if it is the final rally of the game, immediately after the rally.
14.5 If a player stops play during a rally to appeal that the ball is broken only to find subsequently that the ball

is not broken, then that player shall lose that stroke.

15 Warm up
15.1 Immediately preceding the start of play, the Referee shall allow on the court of play a period of 5 minutes to the two players together for the purpose of warming up the ball to be used for the match.

With 2½ minutes of the warm-up remaining, the Referee shall advise the players that they have used half their warm-up time with the call 'half-time' and ensure that they change sides unless they mutually agree otherwise. The Referee shall also advise when the warm-up period is complete with the call of 'time'.

In the event of a player electing to warm up separately on the court of play, the Referee shall allow the first player a period of 3½ minutes and his opponent 2½ minutes. In the case of a separate warm-up, the choice of warming up first or second shall be decided by the spin of a racket.

15.2 Where a ball has been substituted under Rule 14 or when the match is being resumed after considerable delay, the Referee shall allow the ball to be warmed up to playing condition. Play shall resume on the direction of the Referee, or upon mutual consent of the players, whichever is the earlier.

Note to Referees
The Referee must ensure that both players warm up the ball fairly (Rule 15.1 and 15.2). An unfair warm-up shall be dealt with under the provisions of Rule 17.

15.3 Between games the ball shall remain on the floor of the court in view

Rules of the international singles game of squash rackets

and shall not be hit by either player except by mutual consent of the players.

16 Continuity of play After the first service is delivered, play shall be continuous so far as is practical, provided that:

16.1 At any time play may be suspended, owing to bad light or other circumstances beyond the control of the players, for such period as the Referee shall decide. The score shall stand.

If another suitable court is available when the court originally in use remains unsuitable, the match may be transferred to it if both players agree, or as directed by the Referee.

In the event of play being suspended for the day, the score shall stand unless both players disagree in which case the match shall start again.

16.2 An interval of one minute shall be permitted between games and of two minutes between the fourth and fifth games of a five-game match. A player may leave the court during such intervals but shall be ready to resume play by the end of the stated time. When fifteen seconds of the interval permitted between games are left, the Referee shall call 'fifteen seconds' to warn the players to be ready to resume play. At the end of the interval between games the Referee shall call 'time'.

It is the responsibility of the players to be within earshot of the court to hear the calls of 'fifteen seconds' and 'time'.

Notes to Referees
a. Should one player fail to be ready to

resume play when 'time' is called, the Referee shall apply the provisions of Rule 17.
b. Should neither player be ready to resume play when 'time' is called, the Referee shall apply the provisions of Rule 17 for both players.

16.3 If a player satisfies the Referee that a change of equipment, clothing or footwear is necessary, the Referee may allow the player to effect the change as quickly as possible with a maximum allowance of 2 minutes. If the player fails to return within the allotted time, the Referee shall apply the provisions of Rule 17.

16.4 In the event of an injury to a player, the Referee shall decide if it was:
16.4.1 Self-inflicted.
16.4.2 Contributed to accidentally by his opponent, or
16.4.3 Caused by the opponent's deliberate or dangerous play or action.

Notes to Referees
a. In 16.4.2 and 16.4.3 above, the Referee must determine that the injury is genuine.
b. The Referee must not interpret the words 'contributed to accidentally by his opponent' to include the situation where the injury to the player is as a result of that player occupying an unnecessarily close position to his opponent.
c. In Rule 16.4.1 above the Referee shall require the player to continue play; or concede the game, accept the minute interval and then continue play; or concede the match.
d. In Rule 16.4.2 above the Referee shall allow reasonable time for the injured player to recover having regard

to the time schedule of the competition.
e. In Rule 16.4.3 above the Referee shall award the match to the injured player.

16.5 The Referee shall award a stroke, game or match to the opponent of a player, who, in his opinion, persists, after due warning, in delaying the play unreasonably. Such delay may be caused by:
16.5.1 Unduly slow preparation to serve or receive service.
16.5.2 Prolonged discussion with the Referee, or
16.5.3 Delay in returning to the court having left under terms of Rules 16.2 and 16.3.

17 Conduct on court If the Referee considers that the behaviour of a player on court could be intimidating or offensive to an opponent, official or spectator, or could in any other way bring the game into disrepute, the player shall be penalized.

Where a player commits any of the offences listed in the Rules 12.5, 15.2 and 15.3, 16.2, 16.3 or the ISRF Code of Conduct the following penalty provisions may be applied:
Warning by the Referee
Stroke awarded to opponent,
Game awarded to opponent, or
Match awarded to opponent.

Notes to Referees
a. If the Referee stops play to give a warning, a let shall be allowed.
b. If the Referee awards a game, that game shall be the one in progress or the next game if one is not in progress. The offending player shall retain any points already scored in the game awarded.

18 Control of a match A match is normally controlled by a Referee, assisted by a Marker. One person may be appointed to carry out the functions of both Referee and Marker. When a decision has been made by the Referee, he shall announce it to the players and the Marker shall repeat it with the subsequent score.

Notes to Officials

a. Having only one official to carry out roles of both Marker and Referee is undesirable.

b. Up to 30 minutes before the commencement of a match either player may request a referee and/or Marker other than appointed, and this request may be considered and a substitute appointed.

c. Players are not permitted to request any such change(s) after the commencement of a match, unless both agree to do so.

In either case the decision as to whether or not an official is to be replaced must remain in the hands of the tournament Referee or Adjudicator where applicable.

19 Duties of a Marker

19.1 The Marker calls the play followed by the score, with the server's score first. He shall call 'fault', 'foot-fault', 'out', 'not up' or 'down' as appropriate, and shall repeat the Referee's decisions.

19.2 If in the course of play the Marker calls 'not up', 'out', or 'down' or in the case of a second service, 'fault' or 'foot-fault', the rally shall cease.

Note to Markers

If the Marker is unsighted or uncertain he shall make no call.

19.3 Any service or return shall be

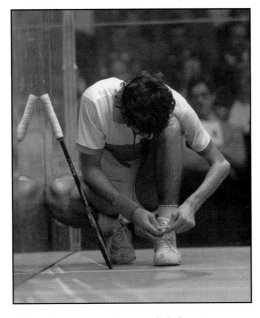

Shoe laces, a universal delaying element not specifically mentioned in the rules of the game

considered good unless otherwise called.

19.4 After the server has served a fault, which has not been accepted for play, the Marker shall repeat the score and the words 'one fault', before the server serves again. This call shall be repeated when the subsequent rally ends one or more times in a let, until the stroke is finally decided.

19.5 If play ceases, and the Marker is unsighted or uncertain, he shall advise the players and shall call on the Referee to make the relevant decision; if the Referee is unable to do so, a let shall be allowed.

19.6 The Marker calls 'hand out' to indicate a change of service.

Note to Markers

Markers must use recognized Marker's calls including when the rally has ceased.

20 Duties of Referee

20.1 The Referee shall allow lets and award strokes; make decisions where called for by the Rules including when a player is struck by the ball and for injuries; and shall decide all appeals, including those against the Marker's calls. The decision of the Referee shall be final.

20.2 The Referee shall not intervene

in the Marker's calling except:

20.2.1 Upon appeal by one of the players.

20.2.2 As provided for in Rules 12 and 17, or

20.2.3 When it is evident that the score has been called incorrectly, in which case he shall have the Marker call the correct score.

Notes to Officials

It is recommended that both Marker and Referee record the score.

20.2.4 If he is certain that the Marker has made an error in stopping play or allowing play to continue, he shall immediately rule accordingly.

20.3 The Referee is responsible for ensuring that all times laid down in the Rules are strictly adhered to.

20.4 The Referee is responsible for ensuring that court conditions are appropriate for play.

20.5 In exceptional cases the Referee may warn a player, award a stroke, a game or the match to the opponent of a player whose conduct is in his opinion detrimental to the match in progress and the game of squash in general. The Referee may also order:

20.5.1 A match to be awarded to a player whose opponent fails to be present on court ready to play, within 10 minutes of the advertised time of play.

20.5.2 Play to be stopped in order to warn that the conduct of one or both of the players is leading to an infringement of the Rules.

Note to Referees

A Referee should avail himself of this Rule as early as possible when either player is showing a tendency to break the provisions of Rules 12, 16.5 or 17.

Rules of the international singles game of squash rackets

Definitions

Adjudicator Responsible for the conduct of players and officials throughout the Tournament.

Appeal A player's request to the Referee to consider an on or off court situation. 'Appeal' is used throughout the Rules in two contexts:
1 where the player requests the Referee to consider varying a Marker's decision and,
2 where the player requests the Referee to allow a let.
Correct form of appeal by player is 'Let Please' or 'Appeal Please'.

Board The Board is the lower horizontal line marking on the front wall, with the 'Tin' beneath it for the full width of the court.

Box (Service) A square delineated area in each quarter court, bounded by part of the short line, part of the side wall and by two other lines and from within which the server serves.

Competition A championship, tournament, league or other competitive match.

Correctly The ball being hit by the racket (held in the hand) not more than once nor with prolonged contact on the racket.

Cut line A line upon the front wall, the top edge of which is 1.83m/6ft above the floor and extending the full width of the court.

Down The expression used to indicate that an otherwise good return has struck the board or has failed to reach the front wall. ('Down' is used as a Marker's call.)

Game Part of a match, commencing with a service by server and concluding when one player has scored or been awarded 9 or 10 points (in accordance with the Rules).

Game-ball The state of the score when server requires one point to win the game in progress. ('Game-ball' is also used as a Marker's call.)

Half-court line A line set upon the floor parallel to the side walls, dividing the back of the court into 2 equal parts, meeting the 'short line' at its midpoint, forming the 'T'.

Half-time The midpoint of the warm-up (also used as a Referee's call).

Hand (As referred to in Rule 9.1.) A player's racket hand position in regard to its approximate location on one side or the other of his body at the moment of ball contact with the racket, a hand on the right side of his body (if facing the front wall) being right and on the left side, left.

Hand in The period from the time a player becomes server until he becomes receiver.

Hand out Condition when change of server occurs. ('Hand-out' is also used as a Marker's call to indicate that a change of hand has occurred.)

Match The complete contest between two players commencing with the warm-up and concluding when both players have left the court at the end of the final rally. (Covers broken ball rule.)

Match-ball The state of the score when the server requires one point to win the match. ('Match-ball' is also used as a Marker's call.)

Not up The expression used to indicate that a ball has not been struck in accordance with the Rules. 'Not up' covers all returns which are not good and are neither 'down' nor 'out' – with the exception of 'faults' and 'foot-faults'. ('Not up' is also used as a Marker's call.)

Out The expression used to indicate that a ball has struck the out line or a wall above such line or the roof, or has passed over any part of the roof (e.g. cross bars). ('Out' is also used as a Marker's call.)

Out line A continuous line comprising the front wall line, both side wall lines and the back wall line and marking the top boundaries of the court.
Note: When a court is constructed without provision of such a line, i.e. the walls comprise only the area used for play, or without the provision of part of such a line (e.g. a glass back wall), and the ball in play strikes part of the horizontal top surface of such a wall and deflects back into court, such a ball is out. Because of the difficulty in ascertaining just where the ball strikes the wall, the decision as to whether such a ball is out should be made by observing the deflection back into court – an abnormal deflection indicating that the ball is out. This decision should be made in the normal manner by the Marker, subject to appeal to the Referee.

Point A unit of the scoring system. One point is added to a player's score when he is server and wins a stroke.

Quarter (Court) One half of the back part of the court which has been divided into two equal parts by the half-court line.

Rally Series of returns of the ball, comprising one or more such returns. A rally commences with a service and concludes when the ball ceases to be in play.

Reasonable backswing The initial action used by a player in moving his racket away from his body as preparation prior to racket movement forward towards the ball for contact. A backswing is reasonable if it is not excessive. An excessive backswing is one in which the player's racket arm is extended towards a straight arm position and/or the racket is extended with the shaft approximately horizontal. The Referee's decision on what constitutes a reasonable as distinct from excessive backswing is final.

Reasonable follow-through The action used by a player in continuing the movement of his racket after it has contacted the ball. A follow-through is reasonable if it is not excessive. An excessive follow-through is one in which the player's racket arm is extended towards a straight arm position with the racket also extended with the shaft horizontal – particularly when the extended position is maintained for other than a momentary period of time. An excessive swing is also one in which the arm extended towards a straight position takes a wider arc than the continued line of flight of the ball, even though the racket shaft is in the correct vertical position. The Referee's decision on what constitutes a reasonable as distinct from excessive follow-through is final.

Referee (Tournament) Tournament Referee is given overall responsibility for all marking and refereeing matters throughout the tournament including the appointment of officials to matches.

Service The method by which the ball is put into play by the server to commence a rally.

Short line A line set out upon the floor parallel to and 5.49m/18ft from the front wall and extending the full width of the court.

Standard The description given to balls, rackets and courts that meet existing ISRF specifications.

Stop Expression used by the Referee to stop play.

Striker The player whose turn it is to hit the ball after it has rebounded from the front wall, or who is in the process of hitting the ball, or who, up to the point of his return reaching the front wall, has just hit the ball.

Stroke The gain achieved by the player who wins a rally either in the normal course of play or on award by the Referee and which results in either the scoring of a point or change of Hand.

Time The expression used by the Referee to indicate that a period of time prescribed in the Rules has elapsed.

Tin Between the board and the floor for the full width of the Court, the tin shall be constructed in such a manner as to make a distinctive noise when struck by the ball.

General note 1: The use of the word 'shall' in the Rules indicates compulsion and the lack of any alternative. The word 'must' indicates a required course of action with considerations to be taken into account if the action is not carried out. The word 'may' indicates the option of carrying out or not carrying out the action.

General note 2: When the words 'he' and 'him' are used in the Rules, they shall be taken to mean 'she' and 'her' as appropriate.

Code of conduct

The following offences may be subject to penalties under Rule 17 and/or disciplinary action:

1 A player who verbally or physically abuses his opponent, the Marker, Referee, Officials, spectators or the sponsors.

2 A player who shows dissent to the Marker, Referee or Officials, including foul or profane language and obscene or offensive gestures.

3 A player who abuses playing equipment or the court.

4 A player who fails to comply with the conditions of entry of a tournament including any rules with regard to clothing or advertising.

5 A player who having entered a tournament or accepted an invitation to play withdraws from the event or fails to attend.

6 A player who fails to complete a match.

7 A player who defaults from a tournament or event. The disciplinary committee may require evidence or proof of 'bona fide' injury, illness or other emergency situation.

8 A player who fails to make himself available to meet reasonable requests for interviews by the media.

9 A player who does not comply with the rules or spirit of the game.

10 A player guilty of any other unreasonable conduct which brings the game into disrepute.

The doubles game

In recent years, the game of doubles squash has grown in popularity at several levels as an extension of activities on singles courts: as a competitive game in its own right; as a training game, sometimes converted to triples where one player, the server, opposes the other two in team until the service is lost and the team splits and reforms against the new server; and as a social game of moderate exercise and great fun.

It should be stressed that doubles squash on singles courts becomes a crowded activity requiring good racket skills and experienced court awareness. It is not a game for beginners or even long-standing players who cannot limit or adapt their swings.

The game was originally conceived for specially constructed doubles courts which are of greater dimensions than singles courts. But few doubles courts remain in the world, for the obvious reason that they take up much more room within a club house. The only doubles court left in Britain, the nation with greater squash facilities than any other, is situated in Edinburgh.

At the professional level, the entertainment element of doubles is recognized by the increasing use of the game as a preliminary or interval activity on finals nights. The English SRA has acknowledged the growing popularity of the game by running British Doubles Championships for both men and women since 1984, with a plate event organized by combining losing players into a mixed doubles competition.

The rules of doubles squash have been adapted, maltreated and sub- jected to various local interpretations over the years of neglect and redis- covery. The English SRA have pro- duced a comprehensive set of rules for the British Championships, how- ever, and it may be useful for players to have a guide to these here.

The basic rules of the international softball game apply to softball dou- bles. There is an American hardball doubles game, but only the scoring system is similar. Outlined below are the main additions and alterations made to the singles rules by the SRA (from whom a complete list may be obtained) which players of doubles squash will need to understand.

Scoring (Rule 2)

The first side to reach fifteen points wins the game. However, if the score becomes 13–13, or 14–14, certain op- tions are open to the side that reaches 13, or 14, first. In the case of a 13–13 scoreline, one of the following must be elected before the next service: a set to five points, with the game finishing at eighteen points; a set to three points, with the game ending at sixteen points; or no set, with the game finishing at fifteen points. If the score reaches 14–14, without a choice having previously been required at 13–13, the alternatives are: a set to three points, with the game ending at seventeen points; or no set.

Service (Rule 4)

The two players in a side serve one after the other, and the order in which they serve should remain constant during the game. (Any change in this order must be made clear at the begin- ning of a game.) The winners of the game can choose either to serve or to receive service to begin the next game, bearing in mind that the first service of every game is taken by the second server only.

The first server can choose to begin serving from either service box; ser- vice then alternates between left and right until side-out or the end of the game. However, there is no penalty attached to serving from the wrong box. Nevertheless, the receiver can demand that the service be taken from the correct box, provided he has not attempted to return it. Similarly, it must be taken from the correct box if the referee calls let before the receiver has attempted a return of service.

In doubles a service is a fault under normal foot-fault and court marking rules, but it is also just a fault if served out above any of the walls. Any com- bination of faults in one service counts only as a single fault, but the receiver is barred from playing a fault of any description.

Return of service (Rule 5)

As with serving, there is a set pattern for return of service. One player must be designated to receive in the right- hand box, the other in the left-hand box. This order, established for each side, must be adhered to during the game, and once again a change can only be made if it is announced at the start of a game.

Let (Rule 6)

A let in doubles, as in singles, will be called in the case of an undecided stroke. However, given the nature of the doubles game, a few sup- plementary rules are observed.

In addition to the let situations of interference and being struck by the

ball, such a decision will
given if the striker refrains from making his shot for fear of injuring an opponent. Similarly, if his racket makes contact with an opponent or his racket before striking the ball, a let may be called even when the stroke has been completed. However, the rally may be continued unless a let is called by either the referee or one of the players.

In the event of the striker following the ball round, turning his body, or letting the ball pass behind him, the let rule should be utilized if this results in him taking the ball on the forehand in the backhand side of the court and vice versa.

Interference and baulk
(Rules 6 and 8)

The normal rules governing interference apply. However, if every effort is made to give an opponent a fair view of the ball, no let will be given when there is interference purely with an opponent's vision as he follows the flight of the ball or when the interference is created by the striker's partner. Both opponents must be given freedom, as far as possible, to play the ball to any part of the front wall or to either side wall near the front wall.

If the referee calls a baulk, play will stop immediately. A baulk decision may be given for one of two reasons. First, if the referee believes that there is unnecessary interference with the striker, in which case the point will go against the offending side; and second, if there is unnecessary crowding, even though an opponent may not actually be prevented from making the shot.

Sue Wright is given room in the backhand court both by her partner, her sister Debbie, and the opposing team, Lisa Opie and Fiona Geaves

Appeals may be made by the players if the referee fails to call either a baulk or a let.

Hitting an opponent with the ball
(Rule 9)

If, before hitting the front wall, the ball makes contact with an opponent, a let is given for interference in the case of a good return. However, the striker's side loses the point if the return would not have been good. Similarly, if a good ball hits the striker's partner, the point goes to the other side.

In the case of a good return that has hit the front wall and then touches any player before being played again and before touching the floor twice, the point is lost by the side of the player touched.

The warm-up (Rule 10)

Players in doubles are given six minutes in which to warm up the ball for matchplay. The players spin a racket to decide which side warms up first; the first side has 3½ minutes, and their opponents 2½ minutes.

Continuity of play (Rule 12)

The interval between games differs slightly in doubles. One minute is allowed between games one and two, and two and three; but two minutes may be taken between the third and fourth, and fourth and fifth games in a five-game match.

Glossary

Angle
A shot which hits the side wall before reaching the front wall. *See also* Reverse angle, Deep angle, Short angle and Boast

Angle of racket face
The racket face may be open, flat or closed. When the racket face is open, the ball will be lifted high; when it is flat, the ball will travel straight; and when it is closed the ball will be directed down. The accuracy of certain shots will be greatly affected by your ability to control the angle of your racket face. For example, it needs to be open to execute a successful lob, but too open and the ball may go out. Similarly, you need to close the racket face to direct the ball towards the nick, but too closed and you may hit the tin or even the floor.

Attacking game
Tactical moves and shots such as the drop which pressurize opponents into making weak returns that can be attacked and hit away to win the rally. Attack constitutes roughly twenty-five per cent of normal play.

Boast
An angle shot played into the nearest side wall on either hand to reach the front wall close to the opposite side wall.

Cockwrist
The action needed to bring the racket into the ready position. Holding the racket with the wrist cocked is essential for generating power through the shot.

Deep angle
The most important angle shot, the deep angle is played from positions deep in the court and is often used as a last line of defence.

Defensive game
Tactical moves and shots such as the lob which are designed to keep the ball in play when under pressure and to allow time to recover the 'T'. Defence represents approximately seventy-five per cent of normal play.

Doubles
A variation on singles squash in which four players take part, two on each team. Conventional singles courts are these days almost invariably used, giving rise to the need for good racket skills and experienced court awareness.

Drive, see Hitting cross-court and Hitting straight

Drop shot
Essentially an attacking shot, the drop is particularly effective when played low over the tin and running close to the side wall, and as a means to end a rally when directed towards the nick. The drop shot can be played off the bounce and off the volley.

Grip
The most common way of holding the racket is the 'shakehands' grip, so called because the action is precisely like that of shaking hands with a friend. The thumb and forefinger of the playing hand form a 'V' on the handle as they curl around the top of it. The other three fingers form a hold-ing vice, with the thumb resting against the top edge of the second finger. Variations on the grip include the 'Pakistani' version and the 'heel control'.

Half volley
When playing a half volley, the ball is hit immediately after impact with the floor and before it rises on the bounce. This is usually a soft drop shot and is achieved by using a closed racket face.

Hitting cross-court
This basic stroke (also known as the cross-court drive) involves hitting the ball from the front of the court so that it travels from the front wall, cross-court, to the side wall beyond the service box. Accurate execution requires the stroke to be played low and with width. Played loosely, so that the ball comes off the front wall high or into the middle of the court, the stroke will provide an opponent with an easy attacking opportunity.

Hitting straight
Probably the first stroke a player will learn, the straight hit involves striking the ball so that it travels directly from the front wall to the back of the court, without hitting the side wall at any time (also known as the straight drive). The aim should be to play the ball away from the centre of the court, and close to the side wall, taking an opponent as far from the 'T' as possible and making it difficult for him to return.

ISRF
The International Squash Rackets

Federation is the recognized world governing body of the sport and incorporates the leading squash-playing nations. Founded in 1967, the ISRF promotes, administrates and legislates on the game.

Lob

The lob is a delicate touch shot usually played defensively. The ball should be played with height and width so that it makes contact with the side wall deep in the court. The lob may be played either cross-court or straight.

Lob serve

A variation on the basic serve. From a balanced position, with an open racket face, the racket is brought up under the ball so that it strikes the front wall high. The ball then rebounds high off the side wall behind the service box and drops close to the side wall in the back of the court.

Nick

The area of the court where the side wall and the floor join. Shots played into the nick are usually winners.

Overhead volley

A volley shot, hit overhead, which is akin to the smash in tennis. The overhead volley is an attacking shot and requires good timing to bring the racket smoothly through the ball.

Positional game

Playing the ball away from an opponent in order to manoeuvre him out of position and thus create opportunities to attack.

Preparation of the racket

Holding the racket in an up-and-ready position in preparation to play the next shot, either forehand or backhand.

Pressure game

Tactics and shots such as the drive which pressurize opponents into making mistakes by depriving them of time. The ball is taken early on the bounce or volleyed, and hit hard.

Return of service

Keeping the ball in play once it has been served. Since points are rarely won outright on the serve, effective returns of service are a useful weapon.

Reverse angle

An angled shot which is played across the body to hit the side wall furthest away from the racket first.

SRA

The Squash Rackets Association is the recognized governing body of the sport in the UK. It fulfils a number of roles including organizing and administrating national competitions, ensuring that the ISRF rules of play and conduct are abided by and fostering the grass roots of the game.

Serve

The serve is the initiator of play. With one foot in the service box, the server puts the ball into play by hitting it against the front wall, between the cut line and the out line, to land in the opposite service quarter. Variations of the serve are achieved by changes of pace and aim.

Short angle

An attacking angle played from positions at the front of the court.

Swing

The controlled, flowing movement of the arm and racket through the ball. The racket should be taken well back to give the fullness of stroke that will control the ball as well as add to the power. Crucial to the swing are smoothness and rhythm.

'T'

The 'T' is located at the point where the short line meets the half-court line and is so called because of its shape. It is the power position of the court since it is the point from which every part of the playing area is most accessible.

Teleball

A ball with reflective inserts developed specially for use under television cameras and on the coloured floors of the new all-transparent showcourts.

Tin

The area on the court 0.48m/19in from the floor on the front wall. If a player hits the ball into the tin during play he loses the rally.

Veteran

A category of player aged over forty-five among men and over forty among women.

Vintage

A category of player aged over fifty-five among men.

Volley

The volley is any shot in which the ball is hit before it bounces. The serve is, therefore, a form of volley.

Index

Numerals in *italics* refer to illustrations

143

Acknowledgements
We would like to thank the following for
supplying photographs for use in the
book:
Dunlop: pages 9, 17
Vivian Grisogono: pages 109, 110, 112
The Leyland & Birmingham Rubber Co
Ltd (Sorbothane): page 18
Reebok: page 18
Andrew Sceats: page 113
W & D Strings: page 9

All other photographs are by Stephen
Line.

Special instructional photographs: Our
thanks to the players Danny Lee, Adrian
Jaski and Melanie Warren Hawkes, and to
Ian McKenzie for directing the
photography and acting as technical
adviser. We are also grateful to the
Gatwick Penta Hotel for allowing us to
use their Leisure Centre squash court
facilities.